WordPress Theme Design

A complete guide to creating professional
WordPress themes

Tessa Blakeley Silver

PUBLISHING

BIRMINGHAM - MUMBAI

WordPress Theme Design

First published: May 2008

Production Reference: 1230508

Published by Packt Publishing Ltd.
32 Lincoln Road
Olton
Birmingham, B27 6PA, UK.

ISBN 978-1-847193-09-4

www.packtpub.com

Cover Image by Vinayak Chittar (vinayak.chittar@gmail.com)

Credits

Author

Tessa Blakeley Silver

Reviewer

Laurens Leurs

Senior Acquisition Editor

David Barnes

Development Editor

Nikhil Bangera

Technical Editor

Mithun Sehgal

Editorial Team Leader

Mithil Kulkarni

Project Manager

Abhijeet Deobhakta

Project Coordinator

Patricia Weir

Indexer

Hemangini Bari

Proofreader

Cathy Cumberlidge

Production Coordinator

Shantanu Zagade

Aparna Bhagat

Cover Work

Aparna Bhagat

About the Author

Tessa Blakeley Silver's background is in print design and traditional illustration. She evolved over the years into web and multi-media development, where she focuses on usability and interface design. Prior to starting her consulting and development company, hyper3media (pronounced hyper-cube media) (`http://hyper3media.com`), Tessa was the VP of Interactive Technologies at eHigherEducation, an online learning and technology company developing compelling multimedia simulations, interactions, and games that met online educational requirements like 508, AICC, and SCORM. She has also worked as a consultant and freelancer for J. Walter Thompson and The Diamond Trading Company (formerly known as DeBeers), and was a Design Specialist and Senior Associate for PricewaterhouseCoopers' East Region Marketing department. Tessa authors several design and web technology blogs. *WordPress Theme Design* is her second book for Packt Publishing.

Table of Contents

Preface

The goal of this title is to explain the basic steps of creating a WordPress theme. This book focuses on the development, creation, and enhancement of WordPress themes, and therefore does not cover general 'how to' information about WordPress and all its many features and capabilities. This title assumes you have some level of understanding and experience with the basics of the WordPress publishing platform. The WordPress publishing platform has excellent online documentation, which can be found at `http://codex.wordpress.org`. This title does not try to replace or duplicate that documentation, but is intended as a companion to it.

My hope is to save you some time finding relevant information on how to create and modify themes in the extensive WordPress codex, help you understand how WordPress themes work, and show you how to design and build rich, in-depth WordPress themes yourself. Throughout the book, wherever applicable, I'll point you to the relevant WordPress codex documentation along with many other useful online articles and sites.

I've attempted to create a realistic WordPress theme example that anyone can take the basic concepts from and apply to a standard blog, while at the same time, show how flexible WordPress and its theme capabilities are. I hope this book's theme example shows that WordPress can be used to create unique websites that one wouldn't think of as 'just another blog'.

What This Book Covers

Chapter 1 Getting Started as a WordPress Theme Designer introduces you to the WordPress blog system and lets you know what you'll need to be aware of regarding the WordPress theme project you're ready to embark on. The chapter also covers the development tools that are recommended and web skills that you'll need to begin developing a WordPress theme.

Chapter 2 Template Design and Approach takes a look at the essential elements you need to consider when planning your WordPress theme design. It discusses the best tools and processes for making your theme design a reality. I explain my own 'Rapid Design Comping' technique and give you some tips and tricks for developing color schemes and graphic styles for your WordPress theme. By the end of the chapter, you'll have a working XHTML and CSS based 'comp' or mockup of your theme design, ready to be coded up and assembled into a fully functional WordPress theme.

Chapter 3 Coding It Up uses the final XHTML and CSS mockup from Chapter 2 and shows you how to add WordPress PHP template tag code to it and break it down into the template pages a theme requires. Along the way, this chapter covers the essentials of what makes a WordPress theme work. At the end of the chapter, you'll have a basic, working WordPress theme.

Chapter 4 Debugging and Validation discusses the basic techniques of debugging and validation that you should be employing throughout your theme's development. It covers the W3C's XHTML and CSS validation services and how to use the FireFox browser and some of its extensions as a development tool, not just another browser. This chapter also covers troubleshooting some of the most common reasons 'good code goes bad', especially in IE, and best practices for fixing those problems, giving you a great-looking theme across all browsers and platforms.

Chapter 5 Your Theme in Action discuss how to properly set up your WordPress theme's CSS style sheet so that it loads into WordPress installations correctly. It also discuss compressing your theme files into the ZIP file format and running some test installations of your theme package in WordPress's administration panel so you can share your WordPress theme with the world.

Chapter 6 WordPress Reference covers key information under easy-to-look-up headers that will help you with your WordPress theme development, from the two CSS class styles that WordPress itself outputs, to WordPress's PHP template tag code, to a breakdown of "The Loop" along with WordPress functions and features you can take advantage of in your theme development. Information in this chapter is listed along with key links to bookmark to make your theme development as easy as possible.

Chapter 7 Dynamic Menus and Interactive Elements dives into taking your working, debugged, validated, and properly packaged WordPress theme from the earlier chapters, and start enhancing it with dynamic menus using the SuckerFish CSS-based method and Adobe Flash media.

Chapter 8 AJAX/Dynamic Content and Interactive Forms continues showing you how to enhance your WordPress theme by taking a look at the most popular methods for leveraging AJAX techniques in WordPress using plugins and widgets. I'll also give you a complete background on AJAX and when it's best to use those techniques or skip them. The chapter also reviews some cool JavaScript toolkits, libraries, and scripts you can use to simply make your WordPress theme appear 'Ajaxy'.

Chapter 9 Design Tips for Working with WordPress reviews the main tips from the previous chapters and covere some key tips for easily implementing today's coolest CSS tricks into your theme as well as a few final SEO tips that you'll probably run into once you really start putting content into your WordPress site.

What You Need for This Book

Essentially, you'll need a code editor, the latest Firefox browser and any other web browsers you'd like your theme to display well in. Most importantly, you'll need an installation of the latest, stable version of WordPress.

WordPress 2.5 requires the following to be installed:

- PHP version 4.3 or greater
- MySQL version 4.0 or greater

For more information on WordPress 2.5's requirements, please browse to:

```
http://wordpress.org/about/requirements/
```

Chapter 1 covers in detail the software, tools, and skills recommended for WordPress theme development.

Who This Book is For

This book can be used by WordPress users or visual designers (with no server-side scripting or programming experience) who are used to working with the common industry-standard tools like PhotoShop and Dreamweaver or other popular graphic, HTML, and text editors.

Regardless of your web development skill-set or level, you'll be walked through the clear, step-by-step instructions, but there are many web development skills and much WordPress know-how that you'll need to be familiar with to gain maximum benefit from this book.

Conventions

In this book, you will find a number of styles of text that distinguish between different kinds of information. Here are some examples of these styles, and an explanation of their meaning.

Code words in text are shown as follows: "In your `index.html` file, add your `css` import link within the header file:"

A block of code will be set as follows:

```
<head>
<title>OpenSource Online Magazine</title>
<script type="text/javascript" src=""></script>
<style type="text/css" media="screen">
@import url("style.css");
</style>
</head>
```

When we wish to draw your attention to a particular part of a code block, the relevant lines or items will be made bold:

```
<head>
<title>OpenSource Online Magazine</title>
<script type="text/javascript" src=""></script>
<style type="text/css" media="screen">
@import url("style.css");
</style>
</head>
```

New terms and **important words** are introduced in a bold-type font. Words that you see on the screen, in menus or dialog boxes for example, appear in our text like this: "In your WordPress go to **Administration | Design | Themes** (or **Administration | Presentation | Themes in 2.3**). There, you'll be able to select the new theme you just duplicated and renamed. (Look carefully! The image is still the **same** as the default theme.)"

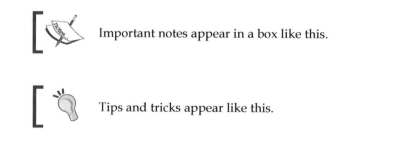

Important notes appear in a box like this.

Tips and tricks appear like this.

Reader Feedback

Feedback from our readers is always welcome. Let us know what you think about this book, what you liked or may have disliked. Reader feedback is important for us to develop titles that you really get the most out of.

To send us general feedback, simply drop an email to feedback@packtpub.com, making sure to mention the book title in the subject of your message.

If there is a book that you need and would like to see us publish, please send us a note in the **SUGGEST A TITLE** form on www.packtpub.com or email to suggest@packtpub.com.

If there is a topic that you have expertise in and you are interested in either writing or contributing to a book, see our author guide on www.packtpub.com/authors.

Customer Support

Now that you are the proud owner of a Packt book, we have a number of things to help you to get the most from your purchase.

Downloading the Example Code for the Book

Visit http://www.packtpub.com/files/code/3094_Code.zip to directly download the example code.

The downloadable files contain instructions on how to use them.

Errata

Although we have taken every care to ensure the accuracy of our contents, mistakes do happen. If you find a mistake in one of our books—maybe a mistake in text or code—we would be grateful if you would report this to us. By doing this you can save other readers from frustration, and help to improve subsequent versions of this book. If you find any errata, report them by visiting http://www.packtpub.com/support, selecting your book, clicking on the **let us know** link, and entering the details of your errata. Once your errata are verified, your submission will be accepted and the errata will be added to the list of existing errata. The existing errata can be viewed by selecting your title from http://www.packtpub.com/support.

Questions

You can contact us at questions@packtpub.com if you are having a problem with some aspect of the book, and we will do our best to address it.

1
Getting Started as a WordPress Theme Designer

Welcome to WordPress theme design! This title is intended to take you through the ins and outs of creating sophisticated professional themes for the WordPress personal publishing platform. WordPress was originally, and is foremost, a blog system. Throughout the majority of this book's chapters—for simplicity's sake—I'll be referring to it as a blog or blog system. But don't be fooled; since its inception, WordPress has evolved way beyond mere blogging capabilities and has many standard features that are expandable with plug-ins and widgets, which make it comparable to a full **CMS (Content Management System)**.

In these upcoming chapters, we'll walk through all the necessary steps required to aid, enhance, and speed your WordPress theme design process. From design tips and suggestions to packaging up the final theme, we'll review the best practices for a range of topics: designing a great theme, rapid theme development, coding markup, testing, debugging, and taking it live.

The last three chapters are dedicated to additional tips, tricks, and various cookbook recipes for adding popular site enhancements to your WordPress theme designs using third-party plug-ins, as well as creating your own custom plug-ins.

WordPress Perks

As you're interested in generating custom themes for WordPress, you'll be very happy to know (especially all you web standards evangelists), that WordPress really does separate content from design.

You may already know from painful experience that many CMS and blog systems end up publishing their content pre-wrapped in (sometimes large) chunks of layout markup (sometimes using table markup), peppered with all sorts of pre-determined selector id and class names.

You usually have to do a fair amount of 'sleuthing' to figure out what these `id` and `classes` are, so that you can create custom CSS rules for them. This is very time consuming.

The good news is, WordPress only publishes two things:

- The site's textual content—the text you enter into the post and the page Administration Panels.
- Supplemental site content wrapped in *list* tags—`<li>` and `</li>`—which usually links to the posts and pages you've entered and the meta information for those items.

That's it! The *list* tags don't even have an ordered or unordered *defining tag* around them. WordPress leaves that up to you. You decide how everything published via WordPress is styled and displayed.

The culmination of all those styling and display decisions along with special WordPress template tags, which pull your site's content into design, are what your WordPress theme consists of.

Does a WordPress Site Have to Be a Blog?

In a nutshell, even before the release of themes in **WordPress 2**, WordPress has been capable of managing static pages and sub-pages since **version 1.5**. Static pages are different from blog posts in that they aren't constrained by the chronology of posts. This means you can manage a wide variety of content with pages and their sub-pages.

WordPress also has a great community of developers supporting it with an ever-growing library of plug-ins. Using plug-ins, you can expand the capabilities of your server-installed WordPress site to include infinite possibilities like event calendars, image galleries, side bar widgets, and even shopping carts. For just about anything you can think of, you can probably find a WordPress plug-in to help you out.

By considering how you want to manage content via WordPress, what kind of additional plug-ins you might employ, and how your theme displays all that content, you can easily create a site that is completely unique and original in concept as well as design.

Again, WordPress was built to be a blog system, and it has some great blog post and category tools. But, if you want to use it to manage a brochure-style site, or have a particular third-party plug-in to be the main feature of your site, and downplay or even remove the blog, that's fine too! You'll just tweak your theme's template files to display your content the way you prefer (which is something you'll be very good at after reading this book).

Pick a Theme or Design Your Own?

I approach theme design from two angles. The first is *Simplicity;* sometimes it suits the client and/or the site to go as bare-bones as possible. In that case, it's quick and easy to take a very basic, pre-made theme and modify it.

The second is *Unique and Beautiful.* Occasionally, the site's theme needs to be created from scratch so that everything displayed caters to the specific kind of content the site offers. This ensures that the site is something eye-catching, which no-one else will have. This is often the best route when custom branding is a priority or you just want to show off your 'Hey, I'm hot-stuff' kind of design skills.

There are many benefits to using or tweaking pre-made themes. First, you save a lot of time getting your site up with a nice theme design. Second, you don't need to know as much about CSS, XHTML, or PHP. This means that with a little web surfing, you can have your WordPress site up-and-running with a stylish look in no time at all.

Drawbacks to Using a Pre-Made Theme

The drawback to using a pre-made theme is that it may not save you as much time as you would hope for. You may realize, even with the new header text and graphic, several other sites may have downloaded and/or purchased it for themselves and you don't stand apart enough.

Perhaps, your site needs a special third-party plug-in for a specific type of content; it might not look quite right without a lot of tweaking. And while we're discussing tweaking, I find that every CSS designer is different and sets up its theme's template files and style sheets accordingly; while it makes perfect sense to them, it can be confusing and time-consuming to work through.

Your approach may have started out as *Simplicity,* but then for one reason or another, you find yourself having to dig deeper and deeper through the theme, and pretty soon it doesn't feel like quick tweaking anymore. Sometimes you realize—for simplicity's sake (no pun intended)—it would have been a whole lot quicker to start from scratch.

Before trying to cut corners with a pre-existing theme, make sure your project really is as *simple* as it claims to be. Once you find a theme, check that you are allowed to tweak and customize it (such as an open-source or creative commons license or royalty free purchase from a template site), and that you have a look at the style sheet and template files. Make sure the theme's assets seem logical and make sense to you.

This Book's Approach

The approach of this book is going to take you through the *Unique and Beautiful* route (or *Unique and Awesome*, whatever your design aesthetics call for) with the idea that once you know how to create a theme from scratch, you'll be more apt at understanding what to look for in other WordPress themes. You'll then be able to assess when it really is better or easier to use a pre-made theme versus building up something of your own from scratch.

Things You'll Need to Know

This book is geared toward visual designers (with no server-side scripting or programming experience) who are used to working with the common industry standard tools like PhotoShop and Dreamweaver or other popular graphic, HTML, and text editors.

Regardless of your web development skill-set or level, you'll be walked through the clear, step-by-step instructions, but there are many web development skills and WordPress know-how that you'll need to be familiar with to gain maximum benefit from this book.

WordPress

Most importantly, you should already be familiar with the most current stable version of WordPress. You should understand how to add content to the WordPress blog system and how its posts, categories, static pages, and sub-pages work. Understanding the basics of installing and using plug-ins will also be helpful (though we will cover that to some extent in the later chapters of the book as well).

Even if you'll be working with a more technical WordPress administrator, you should have an overview of what the WordPress site that you're designing entails, and what—if any—additional plug-ins or widgets will be needed for the project. If your site does require additional plug-ins and widgets, you'll want to have them handy and/or installed in your WordPress development installation (a.k.a **sandbox**—a place to test and play without messing up a live site). This will ensure that your design will cover all the various types of content that the site intends to provide.

What version of **WordPress 2** does this book use? This book focuses on **WordPress 2.5**. It has been an exciting few months to try to write a book for WordPress! When I started writing this book, I was using **WordPress 2.3.2**. I soon upgraded to **2.3.3** and then found myself upgrading again to very much improved version **2.5**. Everything covered in this book has been tested and checked in **WordPress 2.5**. You may occasionally note screenshots from version **2.3.3** being used, but rest assured, any key differences between **2.3.x** and **2.5** are clearly noted when applicable. While this book's case study was developed using version **2.5**, any newer version should have the same core capabilities enabling you to develop themes for it using these techniques. Bug fixes and new features for each new version of WordPress are documented at `http://WordPress.org`.

First time with WordPress? I recommend you read *WordPress Complete* by Hasin Hayder.

CSS

I'll be giving detailed explanations of the CSS rules and properties used in this book, and the 'how and why' behind those decisions. You should know a bit about what CSS is, and the basics of setting up a cascading style sheet and including it within an XHTML page. You'll find that the more comfortable you are with CSS markup and how to use it effectively with XHTML, the better will be your WordPress theme creating experience.

XHTML

You don't need to have every markup tag in the XHTML standard memorized (yes, if you really want, you can still switch to the *Design* view in your HTML editor to drop in those markup tags that you keep forgetting—I won't tell). However, the more XHTML basics you understand, the more comfortable you'll be working in the *Code* view of your HTML editor or with a plain text editor. The more you work directly with the markup, the quicker you'll be able to create well-built themes that are quick loading, semantic, expand easily to accommodate new features, and search engine friendly.

PHP

You definitely don't have to be a PHP programmer to get through this book, but be aware that WordPress uses liberal doses of PHP to work its magic! A lot of this PHP code will be directly visible in your theme's various template files. PHP code is needed to make your theme work with your WordPress installation, as well as make individual template files work with your theme.

If you at least understand how basic PHP syntax is structured, you'll be much less likely to make mistakes while re-typing or copying and pasting code snippets of PHP and WordPress template tags into your theme's template files. You'll be able to more easily recognize the difference between your template files, XHTML, and PHP snippets; so you don't accidentally delete or overwrite anything crucial.

If you get more comfortable with PHP, you'll have the ability to change out variables and call new functions, or even create new functions on your own, again infinitely expanding the possibilities of your WordPress site.

Beef up those web skills! I'm a big fan of the **W3 Schools** site. If you'd like to build up your XHTML, CSS, and PHP understanding, you can use this site to walk you through everything from basic introductions to robust uses of top web languages and technologies. All the lessons are easy, comprehensive and free at `http://w3schools.com`.

Not Necessary, but Helpful

If your project will be incorporating any other special technologies such as JavaScript, AJAX, or Flash content, the more you know and understand how those scripting languages and technologies work, the better it is for your theme making experience (again W3Schools.com is a great place to start).

The more web technologies you have a general understanding of, the more likely you'll be to intuitively make a more flexible theme, which will be able to handle anything the site may need to incorporate into itself in the future.

More of a visual 'see it to do it' learner? lynda.com has a remarkable course selection from the top CSS, XHTML/XML, JavaScript, PHP, and Flash/ActionScript people in the world. You can subscribe and take the courses online, or purchase DVD-ROMs for off-line viewing. The courses might seem pricey at first, but if you're a visual learner (as most designers are), it's money and time well spent. You can have a look at `http://lynda.com`.

Tools of the Trade

In order to get started in the next chapter, you'll need the following tools to help you out:

HTML Editor

You'll need a good HTML editor. DreamWeaver is good; I prefer to use Coda for Mac. When I was on a PC I loved the free text editor HTML-kit (`http://www.htmlkit.com/`), though, any HTML or text editor that lets you enable the following features will work just great (and I recommend you enable all of the following):

- **View line numbers**: This comes in very handy during the validation and debugging process. It can help you find specific lines in a theme file for which a validation tool has returned a fix. This is also helpful for other theme or plug-in instructions given by author, which refer to a specific line of code that needs editing.

- **View syntax colors**: Any worthwhile HTML editor has this feature usually set as a default. The good editors let you choose your own colors. It displays code and other markup in a variety of colors, making it easier to distinguish various types of syntax. Many editors also help you identify *broken* XHTML markup, CSS styles, or PHP code.

- **View non-printing characters**: OK, you might not want this feature turned on all the time. It makes it possible to see hard returns, spaces, tabs, and other special characters that you may or may not want in your markup and code.

- **Text wrapping**: This of course lets you wrap text within the window, so you won't have to scroll horizontally to edit a long line of code. It's best to learn what the key-command shortcut is for this feature in your editor, and/or set up a key-command shortcut for it. You'll find it easier to scroll through unwrapped, nicely-indented, markup and PHP code to quickly get a general overview or find your last stopping point, yet want to turn it on quickly so that you can see and focus your attention on one long line of code.

Graphic Editor

The next piece of software you'll need is a graphic editor. While you can find plenty of CSS-only WordPress themes out there, chances are you'll want to expand on your design a little more and add really nice visual enhancements and effects. These are best achieved by using a graphic editor like Photoshop.

I'll be using Adobe Photoshop in this title, and assume that you have some familiarity with it and working with layers. Any graphic editor you prefer is fine. One that allows you to work with layers is very helpful, especially with the design comping (a.k.a **mockup**) techniques I will suggest in Chapter 2; but you can still get by without layers.

Need a graphic editor? Try GIMP. If you're on a budget and in need of a good image editor, I'd recommend it. It's available for PC, Mac, and Linux. You can get it from `http://gimp.org/`.

Prefer Vector Art? Try Inkscape, which is also available for PC, Mac, and Linux. Bitmap graphic editors are great in that they also let you enhance and edit photographs, but if you just want to create buttons or other interface elements and vector-based illustrations, Inkscape is worth trying out (`http://inkscape.org`).

Firefox

Last, you'll need a web browser. Here, I'm not so flexible. I strongly suggest that you use the latest, stable version of the Firefox browser (`http://mozilla.com/firefox/`).

Why Firefox? I view this browser as a great tool for web developers. It's as essential as my HTML editor, graphics, and FTP programs. Firefox has great features that we'll be taking advantage of to help us streamline the design creation and theme development process. In addition to those built-in features, like the DOM Source Selection Viewer and adhering to CSS2 standards as specified by the W3C, Firefox also has a host of extremely useful extensions like the Web Developer's Toolbar and Firebug, which I recommend to further enhance your work-flow.

Get the extensions: You can get the Web Developer's Toolbar from `https://addons.mozilla.org/en-US/firefox/addon/60`, and Firebug from `https://addons.mozilla.org/en-US/firefox/addon/1843`. Be sure to visit the developer's sites to learn more about each of these extensions.

We'll Be Developing for Firefox First, then IE

In addition to Firefox having all the helpful features and extensions, IE6 and even IE7 have a thing called *quirks mode,* and while Microsoft has attempted a lot of improvements and tried to become more W3C compliant with IE7, there are still some CSS rendering issues.

Your best bet will be to design for Firefox first, and then if you notice things don't look so great in IE6 or IE7, there are plenty of *standardized* fixes and work arounds for those two browsers because their 'wonks' are just that—'wonks' and well-documented.

If you design only looking at one version of IE first, getting your design to look the way you want, then find it a mess in Firefox, Opera, or Safari; you're going to have a much harder time fixing the CSS you made for IE in a more *standards compliant* browser.

Firefox doesn't have to become your only browser. You can keep using IE or any other browser you prefer. I myself prefer Opera for light and speedy web-surfing, but Firefox is one of my key web development tools.

Summary

To get going on your WordPress theme design, you'll want to understand how the WordPress blog system works, and have your head wrapped around the basics of the WordPress project you're ready to embark on. If you'll be working with a more technical WordPress administrator and/or PHP developer, make sure your development installation or sandbox will have the same WordPress plug-ins that the final site needs to have. You'll want to have all the tools that are recommended installed and ready to use as well as brush up on those web skills, especially XHTML and CSS. Get ready to embark on designing a great theme for one of the most popular, open-source, blog systems available for the web today!

2
Theme Design and Approach

In this chapter, we're going to take a look at the essential elements you need to consider when planning your theme design. We'll then move on to discuss the best tools and process for making that design a reality. I'll let you all in on my own 'Rapid Design Comping' strategy and give you some tips and tricks to help you define your color scheme and graphic style, as well as go over some standard techniques for extracting images for your design.

By the end of this chapter, you'll have a working XHTML and CSS based 'comp' or mockup of your WordPress theme's design, ready to be coded up and assembled into a fully functional WordPress theme.

Things to Consider

First up, before we start, I'll acknowledge that you probably already have a design idea in mind and would like to just start producing it. Chances are, unless you're learning theme development solely for yourself, you probably have a client or maybe a website partner who would like to have input on the design. If you have neither, congratulations! You're your own client. Whenever you see me reference 'the client,' just switch your perspective from 'Theme Designer' to 'Website User'.

At any rate, before you start working on that design idea, take a moment to start a checklist and really think about two things: What type of blog the theme is going to be applied to. And what, if any, plug-ins or widgets might be used within the theme.

Types of Blogs

Let's take a look at the following types of blogs (regular sites fit these types as well). These are not *genres*. Within these types of blog sites, just about any genre you can think of—horseback riding, cooking, programming, etc.—can be applied.

You may be designing a theme for a specific site that has a targeted genre. You may want to make a generic theme that anyone can download and use. Still, if you target your theme to fit one of the *types* of blogs below, you might get more downloads of it just because it's more targeted. There's a reason why Brian Gardner's Revolution WordPress Theme is one of the top rated themes for online news and magazine sites (`http://www.revolutiontheme.com/`). People who want to start a magazine or news blog know that this theme will work for their type of site. No need for them to look through dozens or even hundreds of more generic themes, wondering if they can modify it to accommodate their site.

Just read through the following blog types and notice which one of these types your theme fits into. Knowing this will help you determine how the content should be structured and how that might affect your theme's design.

- **The Professional Expert Site**: This is an individual who blogs in their area of expertise to increase their personal exposure and standing. The type of design that can be applied to this site is diverse, depending on the type of expertise and what people's expectations are from that genre. Lawyers will have more people that are just content searchers; the cleaner and more basic the design, the better. Designers need to give the user a great visual experience in addition to the content. People in media might want to create a theme design that lends itself to listening or viewing podcasts.

- **The Corporate Blog**: It's a company that blogs to reach customers and encourage closer relationships, sales, and referrals. Here, the user is actually a content searcher, so you might think a site that's simpler and focuses on text would do better. They just need the specific information about products and services, and maybe would like the opportunity to post a comment to a relevant blog post by the corporation. However, the corporation that is paying you to design the theme is really hoping to further engage the user with a great site experience and immerse them in their brand.

- **Online News Source/Magazine**: This is a blog that provides content on a particular topic, usually funded by ads. The design for this kind of site depends on how traditional the news content is or 'magazinish' the content is. People looking for news and the latest updates in a genre might prefer theme designs that remind them of the experience of reading a news paper, while magazine readers—especially for fashion, travel, people, and 'bleeding-edge' technology—tend to like the site for the design experience of it as well as the content. Just pick up a paper version of any current news source or magazine and you will quickly become aware of what people in that genre are expecting.

- **The Campaign Blog**: These are the non-profit blogs run by charities or 'causes'. The information needs to be structured for clarity and winning people over to understanding and campaigning the cause or candidate. Most users will be content searchers and while being appreciative of a nice clean content structure and design experience, depending on the campaign or cause, users may become critical if the site is too well designed: 'This is nice, but is it where they spend the money I donate, instead of the cause!?'

Keeping the discussed items in consideration, you can now think about the design you have in mind and assess how appropriate it is for the type of blog or site, the kind of experience you want to give to users, as well as what you might think of the user's expectation about what the content and experience should be like.

Plug-ins and Widgets

The second consideration you'll want to make is about plug-ins and widgets. Plug-ins are special files that make it easy to add extra functions and features to your WordPress site. Widgets are now built into WordPress2 and are basically things you can put into your WordPress site's sidebar, regardless of knowing any HTML or PHP.

Plugins and Widgets usually place requirements on a theme: Certain CSS classes will be generated and placed into the site for headers or special text areas. Maybe a template file in the theme might need some specific PHP code to accommodate a plug-in. You'll need to find out the theme requirements of any plug-in or widget that you plan to use, so that you may accommodate it when you code up your theme.

What kinds of plug-ins are available? You can see all the types of plug-ins available on the WordPress.org site , identifying them by their tags (http://wordpress.org/extend/plugins/tags/).

Find out more about widgets: You'll be able to see a sample of widgets, as well as find out the requirements for a widget compatible theme at http://widgets.wordpress.com/. This will walk you through 'widgetizing' (our theme in Chapter 8).

When you begin working on your design, you'll want to compare your sketches and design comp(s) against your plug-ins and widgets checklist, and make sure you're accommodating them.

Getting Ready to Design

[**Design Comp** (abbreviation used in design and print): A preliminary design or sketch is a 'comp,' comprehensive artwork, or composite. It is also known as comp, comprehensive, mockup, sample, or dummy.]

You may already have a design process similar to the one I detail next; if so, just skim what I have to say and skip down to the next main heading. I have a feeling, though, that many of you will find this design comping technique a bit unorthodox, but bear with me, it really works.

Here's how this process came about. Whether or not you design professionally for clients or for yourself, you can probably identify with parts of this experience:

We Have a Problem

Up until a couple of years ago, in order to mockup a site design, I loaded up Photoshop and began a rather time-consuming task of laying down the design's graphical elements and layout samples, which entailed managing, what sometimes ended up being, a *very large* amount of layers, most of which were just lots of text boxes filled with Lorem Ipsum sample text.

I'd show these mockups to the client, they'd make changes, which more often than not were just to the *text* in the mockup, not the overall layout or graphical interface. As my 'standard design procedure' was to have the client approve the mockup *before* production, I'd find myself painstakingly plodding through all my Photoshop text layers, applying the changes to show the mockup to the client again.

Sometimes, I would miss a small piece of text that should have been updated with other sets of text! This would confuse (or annoy) the client and they'd request another change! I guess they figured that as I had to make the change anyway, they might request a few more tweaks to the design as well, which again, were usually more textual than graphical and took a bit of focus to keep track of.

The process of getting a design approved became tedious, and at times, drove me nuts. At one point, I considered dropping my design services and just focusing on programming and markup so that I wouldn't have to deal with it anymore.

It Gets Worse

Upon *finally* getting an approval and starting to produce the design comp into XHTML and CSS, no matter how good I got at CSS and envisioning how the CSS would work while I was mocking-up the layout in Photoshop, I would inevitably include something in the layout that would turn out to be a bit harder than I'd thought to be to reproduce with XHTML and CSS.

I was then saddled with two unappealing options: either go back to the client and get them to accept a more reasonable 'reality' of the design; or spend *more time* doing all sorts of tedious research and experimentation with the XHTML and CSS to achieve the desired layout, or other effect, across all browsers and IE.

The Solution–Rapid Design Comping

I soon realized the problem was me hanging onto a very antiquated design process of what the *mockup* was and what *production* was. Before late 2005, I would have never cracked open my HTML editor without a signed design approval from the client, but why?

The web was originally made for text. Thus, it has a very nice, robust markup system for categorizing that text (a.k.a. HTML/XTHML). Now with browsers that all comply (more or less) to CSS standards, the options for displaying those marked-up items are more robust, but there are *still* limitations.

Photoshop, on the other hand, has no display limitations. It was made to edit and enhance digital photographs and create amazing visual designs. It can handle anything you layout into it, be it realistic for CSS or not. It *was not* designed to help you effectively manage layers upon layers of text that would be best handled with global stylings!

This realization led me to the ten step process I've termed **Rapid Design Comping**. The term is a bit of a play on the term **Rapid Prototyping** which had become very popular at the time this design process emerged for me, which is indeed inspired by, and bears some similarities to Rapid Prototyping.

The following is the overview; we'll go over each step in detail afterwards:

1. **Sketch It**: Napkins are great! I usually use the other side of a recycled piece of photocopied paper—the more basic the better. No fine artist skills required! **Perk**: Using this sketch you can not only get your graphic interface ideas down, but you can already start to think about how the user will interact with your theme design and re-sketch any new ideas or changes accordingly.

2. **Start with the Structure**: I create an ideal, un-styled semantic XHTML document structure and attach a bare bones CSS sheet to it.

3. **Add the Text**: Lots of text, the more the better! A sample of actual content is best, but Lorem Ipsum is fine too.

4. **CSS Typography**: Think of your *Typography* and assign your decisions to the stylesheet. Review! Don't like how the formatted text looks *in-line*? Being separated into columns with fancy background graphics won't make it any better. Get your text to look nice and read well *now* before moving on to layout.

5. **CSS Layout**: Set up the *Layout*—this is where you'll see upfront if your layout idea from your sketch will even work. Any problems here and you can re-think the design's layout into something more realistic (and usually more clean and elegant). **Perk**: Your client will *never* see, much less become attached to, a layout that would cause you problems down the road in CSS.

6. **CSS Color Scheme**: Assign your color scheme basics to the CSS. We're close to needing Photoshop anyway, so you might as well open it up. I sometimes find it useful to use Photoshop to help me come up with a color scheme and get the hex numbers for the stylesheet.

7. **Take a Screenshot**: Time for Photoshop! Paste the screenshot of your basic layout into your Photoshop file.

8. **Photoshop**: Have *fun* creating the graphical interface elements that will be applied to this layout over your screenshot.

9. **Send for Approval**: Export a `.jpg` or `.png` format of the layout and send it to the client. **Perk**: If the client has text changes, just make them in your CSS (which will update your text globally—no layer hunting for all your headers or links, etc.) and resnap a screenshot to place back in the Photoshop file with the graphic elements. If they have a graphical interface change, well that's what Photoshop does best! Make the changes and resend for approval.

10. **Production**: Here's the best part; you're more than halfway there! Slice and export the interface elements you created over (or under) your screenshot and apply them with the background image rules in your CSS. Because you worked directly over a screenshot of the layout, slicing the images to the correct size is easier and you won't discover that you need to tweak the layout of the CSS as much to accommodate the graphic elements.

> If you start getting really good and speedy with this process, and/or especially if you have text overlaying the complicated backgrounds, you can also just export your images to your CSS file right away and send the client a straight screenshot from the browser to approve. Play with this process and see what works best for you.

For the purposes of this title, there's actually an eleventh step of production, which is, of course, coding and separating up that produced mockup into your WordPress Theme. We'll get to that in Chapter 3.

Let's Get Started

After taking all of the preceding items into consideration, I've decided that the type of theme I'd like to create, and the one we'll be working on throughout this book, is going to be an **Online News Source/Magazine** type of site. Our site's content will be geared towards using **Open-Source Software**. Even though this type of site usually does very well by just focusing on the content, I would like to give the users the design experience of reading a more trendy paper magazine.

Sketch It

The whole point of this step is to just get your layout down along with figuring out your graphic element scheme. You don't have to be a great artist or technical illustrator As you'll see next, I'm clearly no DaVinci! Just put the gist of your layout down on a sheet of paper, quickly!

The best place to start is to reference your checklist from the steps I provided, which consider how the site is going to be used. Focus on your desired layout: Are you going to have columns? If so, how many? On the left or the right? How tall is your header? Will your footer be broken into columns? All of these things will compose the structure of your design. You can then move on to any graphic element schemes you might have in mind; that is, would you use rounded corners on the box edges or a particular icon set? Where? How often?

In the following figure, I've sketched a basic three column layout which features using the WordPress blog to manage and feature magazine-style articles on a particular subject, rather than just straight-up blog posts.

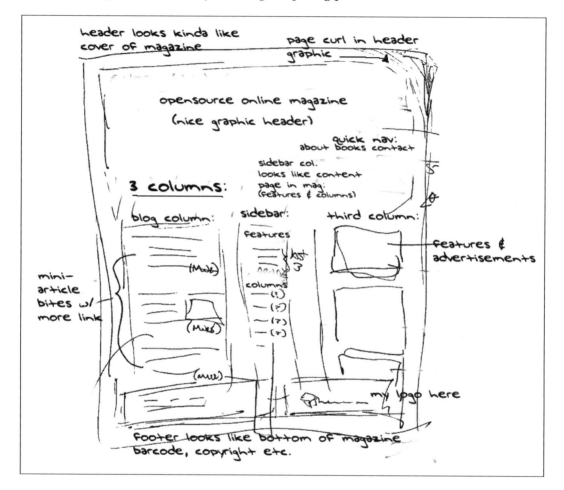

Because the design experience I want to give my site's viewers will be that of reading a paper magazine, the scheme for my graphic elements are going to focus on creating the illusion of paper edges and columned magazine-style layouts (particularly on the home page). I want the home page to feel like similar to the 'Table of Contents' page in a magazine.

TOC's in magazines usually have big images and/or intro text to the featured articles to peak your interest. They then have listings of recurring 'columns' like, 'Ask the Expert' or 'Rants and Raves' (things like that).

Therefore, the graphical element scheme of my site, which will make up the majority of the design experience, will focus on 'paper edges', curling up at the corners, like a well-read, glossy, thin magazine paper tends to do. My layout is going to take advantage of the main WordPress blog, using the pre-snips of the story as the intro text to peak interest. I'll use WordPress's *categorizing* feature to mimic a display of recurring columns (as in recurring articles) and the *monthly archive list* as a 'Past Issues' list.

Consider Usability

Once you've created your sketch, based on your considerations, look at it for usability. Imagine you are someone who has come to the site for the information it contains.

What do you think the user will actually do? What kind of goals might they have for coming to your site? How hard or easy will it be for them to attain those goals? How hard or easy do you *want it to be* for them to attain those goals?

Are you adhering to standard web conventions? If not, have you let your user know what else to expect? Web standards and conventions are more than what's laid out in a lengthy W3C document. A lot of them are just adhering to what we, as web users expect. For example, if text has underlines in it and/or is a different color, we expect that text to be a link. If something looks like a button, we expect clicking on it to do something, like process the comment form we just filled out or adding an item to our cart.

It's perfectly OK to get creative and break away from the norm and not use all the web conventions. But be sure to let your viewers know *upfront* what to expect, especially as most of us are simply expecting a web page to act like a web page!

Looking at your sketch, do any of the just discussed scenarios make you realize any revisions need to be made? If so, it's pretty easy to do. Make another sketch!

Clean it up? This might seem to defeat the purpose of 'Rapid Design Comping', but if you're working within a large design team, you may need to take an hour or so to clean your sketch up into a nicer line drawing (sometimes called a 'wire frame'). This may help other developers on your team more clearly understand your WordPress theme idea.

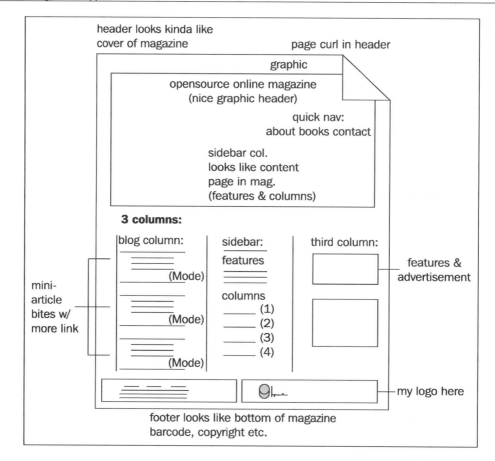

Start with the Structure

The preceding usability scenarios deal with someone who will be looking at your content through your fully CSS stylized WordPress theme. What if someone views this content in a mobile browser? A text-only browser? Or a text-to-speech browser? Will the un-styled content still be understood? Or, will someone be scrolling or worse, *listening* and trying to tab through thirteen minutes of your sidebar 'blogroll' or Flickr image links before getting to the page's main content? To ensure such a scenario doesn't happen, we'll dive into our design comp by starting with the XHTML structure.

Open up your HTML or text editor and create a new, fresh `index.html` page.

The DOCTYPE

XHTML has two common DOCTYPEs: **Strict** and **Transitional**. There's also the newer **1.1** DOCTYPE for 'modularized' XHTML. The Strict and 1.1 DOCTYPE is for the truly semantic. It's requirements suggest you have absolutely no presentational markup in your XHTML (though in Strict 1.0, any `strong`, `em`, `b`, `i`, or other presentation tags that slip in, will still technically validate on W3C's service; it's just not the recommendation for how to remain 'Strict').

You can use what you like, especially if it's your WordPress site. However, if the WordPress site will not remain completely under your control, you can't control everything that other authors will add to the posts and pages. It's safest to use the `Transitional 1.0 DOCTYPE` which will keep your theme valid and have more flexibility for different kinds of users and the type of content they place into the system.

For our OpenSource Magazine theme, I'll go ahead and use the 1.0 Transitional DOCTYPE:

```
<!DOCTYPE html PUBLIC "-//W3C//DTD XHTML 1.0 Transitional//EN"
"http://www.w3.org/TR/xhtml1/DTD/xhtml1-transitional.dtd">
```

You should note, while being integral to a valid template, the DOCTYPE declaration itself is not a part of the XHTML document or an XHTML element. It does not use a closing tag, even though it does look a bit like an empty tag.

> **Check your editor's preferences**! Some editors automatically place a DOCTYPE and the required `html`, `header`, `title`, and body tags into your document when you open up your blank file. That's great, but please go into your editor's preferences and make sure your **Markup** and **DTD** preferences are set to **XHTML** and **Transitional** (or **Strict**, if you prefer). Some editors that offer a 'design' or WYSIWYG view will overwrite the DOCTYPE to whatever the preferences are set to, when you switch between the **Design** and **Source** (a.k.a. **Code**) views. Dreamweaver doesn't seem to have this problem, but you should set your DOCTYPE preferences there too, just to be safe.

The Main Body

After our DOCTYPE, we can add in the other essential requirements of an XHTML file, which are as follows:

```
<html xmlns="http://www.w3.org/1999/xhtml" xml:lang="en" lang="en">
<head>
<title>My New Theme Title</title>
</head>
<body> body parts go here </body>
</html>
```

Attach the Basic StyleSheet

At this time, as we have our basic header tags created, I go ahead and attach a bare bones stylesheet. This stylesheet just has the general items, matching `div id`'s and placeholders that I use for most CSS styling. But it's just the 'shell'. There are no display parameters for any of the rules.

Time For Action:

1. In your `index.html` file, add your `css` import link within the header file:

```
<head>
<title>
    OpenSource Online Magazine</title>
    <script type="text/javascript" src=""></script>
    <style type="text/css" media="screen">
    @import url("style.css");
    </style>
</head>
```

2. Create a `style.css` file and include this basic shell:

```
/*
Enter WP Design & Creation Comments Here
*/
/*////////// GENERAL //////////*/
body {}
#container {}
#container2 {}
#container3 {}
/*////////// TYPEOGRAPHY //////////*/
h1 {}
h2 {}
h3 {}
h4 {}
p {}
a {}
a:hover {}
a:visited {}
/*////////// HEADERS //////////*/
#header {
    /*background: #666666;url("images/css_cs_header.jpg") no-repeat
    left top;*/
}
#header p, #header h1, #header h2/**/ {
    /*display: none;*/
```

```
}
/*////////// CONTENT //////////*/
#content {}
/*////////// SIDEBARS //////////*/
#sidebarLT {}
#sidebarRT {}
/*////////// NAV //////////*/
#top_navlist {}
/*////////// BLOG ELEMENTS //////////*/
/*////////// FORMS //////////*/
/*////////// FOOTER //////////*/
#footer {}
/*////////// IMAGES //////////*/
/*////// FUN CLASSES //////////*/
/*any little extra flares and fun design
elements you want to add can go here*/
```

Basic Semantic XHTML Structure

Referring back to our sketch, we'd like our theme to have a standard header that stretches across three columns. The left column being the main content or blog posts; the middle column being our side bar; and a third column on the far right that will hold our own custom feature links and/or advertisements. A footer will run across the bottom of all three columns, naturally falling beneath the longest extending column, no matter which of the three it is.

So let's start off with some very basic code within our <body> tag to get that going. I've included relevant id names on each div in order to keep track of them and later to assist me with my CSS development.

```
<body>
<a name="top"></a><!--anchor for top-->
<div id="container"><!--container goes here-->
<div id="header">
<em>Header:</em> background image and text elements for header will go
inside this div
</div><!--//header-->
<!-- Begin #container2 this holds the content and sidebars-->
<div id="container2">
<!-- Begin #container3 keeps the left col and body positioned-->
<div id="container3">
<!-- Begin #content -->
```

```
<div id="content">
<em>Main Content:</em> Post content will go here inside this div
</div><!-- //content -->

<!-- #left sidebar -->
<div id="sidebarLT">
<em>Left Side Bar:</em> Will contain WordPress content related links
</div><!--//sidebarLT  -->
</div><!--//container3-->

<!-- #right sidebar -->
<div id="sidebarRT">
<em>Right Side Bar:</em> This will include additional ads,
or non-content relevant items.
</div><!--//sidebarRT -->

<div id="pushbottom"> </div><!--//this div will span across the 3 divs
above it making sure the footer stays at the bottom of the longest
column-->

</div><!--//container2-->

<div id="top_navlist">
<em>Top Nav:</em> For reading through straight text, it's best to have
links at bottom (css will place it up top, for visual ease of use)
</div><!--//top_navlist-->

<div id="footer">
<em>Footer:</em> quick links for CSS design users who've had to scroll
to the bottom plus site information and copyright will go here

</div><!--//footer-->

</div><!--//container-->

</body>
```

Header: background image and text elments for header will go inside this div.
Main Content: Post content will go here inside this div.
Left Side Bar: Will contain WordPress content related links
Right Side Bar: This will include additional ads, or non-content relevant items.
Top Nav: For reading through straight text, it's best to have links at bottom (css will place it up top, for visual ease of use)
Footer: quick links for CSS design users who've had to scroll to the bottom plus site information and copyright will go here

Not much to look at, but you can see our semantic goals at work. For instance, if a search engine bot or someone using a text-only browser or mobile device arrived and viewed our site, the following is the order they'd see things in:

- *Header*—because it's good to know whose stuff you're looking at.
- *Main Content*—get right to the point of what we're looking for.
- *Left Column Content*—under the main content, should have the next most interesting items—Features list, Category a.k.a. Columns links, and Archives a.k.a. 'Past Issues' links.
- *Right Column Content*—secondary information such as advertisements and non-content related items.
- *TopPage Navigation* – even though in the design this will be on the top, it's best to have it at the bottom in text-only viewing.
- *Footer Information*—if this was a page of real content, it's nice to see whose site we're on again, especially if we've been scrolling or crawling down for some time.

Moving navigation to the bottom: Some SEO experts believe that another reason to semantically push the navigation items down the page after the body of content as far as possible is, it encourages the search engine bots to crawl and index more of the page's content before wandering off down the first link it comes to. The more content the bot can index at a time, the sooner you'll be displayed with it on the search engine. Apparently, it can take months before a site is fully indexed, depending on its size. I have no idea if this is actually true, but it's in-line with my semantic structure based on usability, so no harm done. You'll have to tell us at Packt Publishing if you think your content is getting better SE coverage based on this structure.

Adding Text–Typography

We're now ready to make our typography considerations. Even if you're designing far into the experience side of the scale, text is the most common element of a site, so you should be prepared to put a fair amount of thought into it.

Start with the Text

I like to add an amount of text that has a site name and description paragraph right on top in my header tags, the main body text up high in the content tags, secondary then tertiary text below that (some of which usually ends up in a side bar), and the navigation at the very bottom of the page in an unordered list. You know, it's basically that 'perfect page' SEO experts go on and on about—a Google bot's delight, if you will.

Minimally, I include `<h1>`, `<h2>`, `<h3>`, and `<h4>` headers along with links, strong and emphasized text, as well as a block-quote or two. If I know for sure that the site will be using the specific markup like `<code>` or form elements like `<textarea>` or `<input>`, I try to include examples of text wrapped in these tags as well. This will help me ensure that I create style rules for all the possible markup elements.

To help me out visually, I do tweak the text a bit to fit the situation for WordPress theme designing. I put some blog post-ish stuff in there along with example text of features I want the blog to have, that is, 'read more' links or a 'how many comments' display along with samples of what kind of links the blog system will provide.

Actually, start with a lot of text. Here's my secret: I use a lot of sample text. A major issue I've always noticed about design comps and reality is this: We tend to create a nice mockup that's got clean little two-word headers followed by trim and tight, one or two sentence paragraphs (which are also easier to handle if you did the entire mockup in Photoshop).

In this optimally minimalist sample, the design looks beautiful. However, the client then dumps all their content into theme which includes long, boring, two sentence headlines and reams and reams of unscannable text. Your beautiful theme design now seems dumpy and all of a sudden the client isn't so happy, and they want you to incorporate full of suggestions in order to compensate for their text-heavy site.

Just design for lots of text upfront. If the site ends up having less text than what's in your comp, that's perfectly fine; less text will always look better. Getting mounds of it to look good after the fact is what's hard.

```
┌─────────────────────────────────────────────────────────────────────────┐
│ ○ ○ ○              OpenSource Online Magazine with Typeography            │
│ ⊘ Disable ▾  ⚖ Cookies ▾  ▣ CSS ▾  ▤ Forms ▾  ▣ Images ▾  ⓘ Information ▾  ⊛ Miscellaneous ▾  ✎ Outline ▾  ⋮ Resize ▾  ⚲ Tools ▾  ▣ View Source ▾  ⌗ Optio │
```

Header: OpenSource Online Magazine

Using Open Source for work and play

Content: This Month

Really Long Article Title Name The More Text The Better Cause You Never Know

by Author Name for Column Type

Lorem ipsum dolor sit amet, consectetuer adipiscing elit. Sed a eros nec orci volutpat vestibulum. Ut pellentesque sagittis metus. In euismod tellus id ante. Ut lectus. Nunc adipiscing. Praesent luctus, massa quis vulputate rhoncus, justo turpis mollis dolor, nec blandit nisl mauris et pede.

Lorem ipsum dolor sit amet, consectetuer adipiscing elit. Sed a eros nec orci volutpat vestibulum. Ut pellentesque sagittis metus.

Read the rest of this entry »

No Comments Add Your Thoughts

Left Sidebar: Features

- Article Name 01 Lorem ipsum dolor sit amet consectetuer adipiscing elit
- Article Name 02 Lorem ipsum dolor sit amet
- Article Name 03 Lorem ipsum

Columns

- Name of Category 01 Lorem ipsum dolor sit amet consectetuer
- Name of Category 02 Lorem ipsum dolor sit amet
- Name of Category 03 Lorem ipsum dolor sit amet consectetuer adipiscing elit.

Past Issues

- Archive Link year/month 01
- Archive Link year/month 02
- Archive Link year/month 03

Right Sidebar: Key BlockQuotes, links, adds other items.

main navigation

- link 01
- link 02
- link 03

Footer Information

link 01 | link 02 | link 03 | link 04 | link 05

OpenSource Online Magazine is proudly powered by WordPress

```
Done
```

Font Choices

When it comes to fonts on the web, we're limited. You must design for the most common fonts that are widely available across operating systems. It doesn't mean you shouldn't spend time really considering what your options are.

I think about the type of information the site holds, what's expected along with what's in vogue right now. I then consider my fonts and mix them carefully. I usually think in terms of headers, secondary fonts, block-quotes, specialty text (like depicting code), and paragraph page text.

You can use any fonts you want as long as you think there's a really good chance that others will have the same font on their computers. Here is a list of the basic fonts I mix and match from and why:

- **San-Serif Fonts**: These fonts don't contain 'serifs' (hence the name san-serif). Serifs are the little 'feet' you see on the appendages of type faces. San-Serif fonts are usually considered more *new* and *modern*.

- **Verdana**: This font is common on every platform and was specifically designed for web reading at smaller web sizes. When you really want to use a san-serif font for your body text, this is your best bet. (There was a great article in The New Yorker in 2007 about the designer of this font.)

- **Arial and Helvetica**: Common on every platform. A little tame. Great for clean headlines, but a bit hard to read at smaller font sizes.

- **Trebuchet**: Fairly common nowadays, and a pretty popular font on the 'web 2.0' styled sites. Clean like Arial with a lot more character. It reads a little better at smaller sizes than Arial. This was originally a Microsoft font, so sometimes it doesn't appear in older Mac or Linux OSs (Verdana is a MS font too, originally released with IE 3, but its design for screen readability got it opted quickly by other OSs).

- **Century Gothic**: Fairly common. Clean and round, a nice break from the norm. Reads terribly at small sizes though. Use for headings only.

- **Comic Sans Serif**: Another MS font, but common on all platforms. Fun and friendly, based on traditional comic book hand lettering. I've never been able to use it in a design (I do try from time to time, and feel it's 'hokey'), but I always admire when it's used well in site design (See Chapter 9 for a great example).

- **Serif Fonts**: These fonts are considered more traditional, or 'bookish', as serif fonts were designed specifically to read well in print. The serifs (those 'little feet') on the appendages of the letters form subtle lines for your eyes to follow.

- **Times New Roman and Times**: Very common on all platforms; one of the most common serif fonts. Comes off very traditional, professional, and/or serious.

- **Georgia**: Pretty common, again predominately a Microsoft font. I feel it has a lot of character, nice serifs, and a big and fat body. Like Verdana, Georgia was specifically designed for on-screen reading for any size. Comes off professional, but not quite as serious as Times New Roman.

- **Century Schoolbook**: Pretty common. Similar to Georgia, just not as 'fat'.

- **Courier New**: This is a mono-spaced font, based on the old typewriters and often what your HTML and text editor prefers to display (the point of mono-type is that the characters don't merge together, so it's easier to see your syntax). As a result of that association, I usually reserve this font for presenting code snippets or technical definitions within my designs.

Cascading Fonts

When assigning font-families to your CSS rules, you can set up backup font choices. This means that if someone doesn't happen to have Century Schoolbook, then they probably have Georgia, and if they don't have Georgia either, then they definitely have Times New Roman, and if they don't have that? Well, at the very least you can rely on their browser's built-in 'generic' assigned font. Just specify: `serif`, `sans-serif`, or `mono-space`.

Because I want the style of my site's text to convey *friendly* and modern *magazinish* look, I'm going to have my headers be a mix of Trebuchet and Georgia, while the body content of my text will be Trebuchet as well. My font-families will look something like the following:

For body text:

```
#container {
    font-family: "Trebuchet MS", Verdana, Arial, Helvetica, sans-serif;
}
```

For h1 and h4 headers:

```
h1, h4 {
    font-family: "Trebuchet MS", Arial, Helvetica, sans-serif;
}
```

For h2 and h3 headers:

```
h2, h3{
font-family: Georgia, Times, serif;
}
```

Font Sizing

Thankfully, we seem to be out of the trend where intsy-teensy type is all the rage. I tend to stick with common sense: Is the body text readable? Do my eyes flow easily from header to header? Can I scan through the body text landing on emphasized or bolded keywords, links, and sub-headers? If so, I move onto the next step.

Where I can't help you is determining *how* to size your fonts. The W3C recommends using em sizing for fonts on web pages. I, who normally treat anything the W3C recommends as scripture, actually use (gasp!) pixels to size my fonts.

Why? Because it's simpler and quicker for *me* to work with. This might not be the case for you, and that's fine. Yes, I've read the evidence and understood the logic behind em sizing. But, I usually design my sites for FireFox, IE6 and IE7, Opera 9, and Safari 3 (in about that order of importance). All these browsers seem to resize pixel-sized fonts and line-heights just fine. I also tend to design my sites with locked widths, assuming vertical expansion. Resizing fonts up or down from within any of these browsers may not look wonderful, but it does not *break* any of my designs, it just gives you bigger text to read and a little more scrolling to do.

You may not agree with using pixels to size, and if you intend for your theme's layouts to be flexible and resizable, then you'll definitely want to go with em sizing (for a lot of elements, not just your fonts).

You can set your font sizes to anything you'd like. I've set my container and heading rules to the following:

```
#container {
  font-family: "Trebuchet MS", Verdana, Arial, Helvetica, sans-serif;
  font-size: 12px;
}
h1 {
  font-size: 32px;
}
h2 {
  font-size: 22px;
}
h3 {
  font-size: 16px;
}
h4 {
  font-size: 14px;
}
```

Want more info on the pros and cons of em and pixel sizing? A List Apart has several great articles on the subject. The two that are most relevant are: **How to Size Text in CSS** (http://www.alistapart.com/articles/howtosizetextincss) and **Setting Type on the Web to a Baseline Grid** (http://www.alistapart.com/articles/settingtypeontheweb).

Really interested in web typography? Be sure to check out http://webtypography.net/.

Paragraphs

No matter what sizing method you decide on, px or em, be sure to give in some space. With just the right amount of space between the lines, the eye can follow the text much more easily, but not too much space should be given! By setting your line-heights to a few more pixels (or em percentages) more than the 'auto' line-height for the font size, you'll find the text much easier to scan online. Also, add a little extra margin-bottom spacing to your paragraph rule. This will automatically add a natural definition to each paragraph without the need for adding in hard return breaks (<br/>). You'll need to experiment with this on your own, as each font family will work with different line-height settings and font sizes.

I've set my container rule to have a line-height of 16px and my paragraph rule to allow a bottom margin of 18px:

```
#container {
    font-family: "Trebuchet MS", Verdana, Arial, Helvetica, sans-serif;
    font-size: 12px;
    line-height:16px;
}
p {
    margin-bottom: 18px;
}
```

Default Links

Many of the links in our theme are going to be custom-designed, based on the div id they are located in. Still, I've gone ahead and decided to adjust my basic link or a: href settings. I like my links to be bold and stand out, but not have what I find to be, a distracting underline. However, I do feel the underline is an essential part of what people expect a link to have, so if they do decide to move the mouse over to any of the bold text, an underline will appear and they'll immediately know it's a link.

I've set the bold and underline for my links like the following:

```
a {
    text-decoration: none;
    font-weight: bold;
}
a:hover {
    text-decoration: underline;
}
```

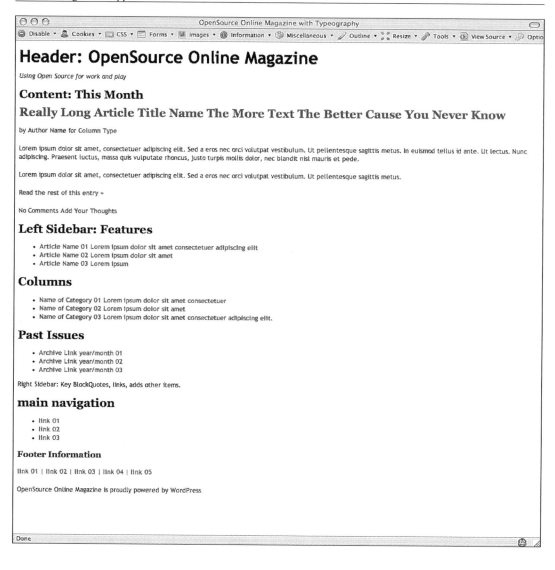

Header: OpenSource Online Magazine

Using Open Source for work and play

Content: This Month

Really Long Article Title Name The More Text The Better Cause You Never Know

by Author Name for Column Type

Lorem ipsum dolor sit amet, consectetuer adipiscing elit. Sed a eros nec orci volutpat vestibulum. Ut pellentesque sagittis metus. In euismod tellus id ante. Ut lectus. Nunc adipiscing. Praesent luctus, massa quis vulputate rhoncus, justo turpis mollis dolor, nec blandit nisl mauris et pede.

Lorem ipsum dolor sit amet, consectetuer adipiscing elit. Sed a eros nec orci volutpat vestibulum. Ut pellentesque sagittis metus.

Read the rest of this entry »

No Comments Add Your Thoughts

Left Sidebar: Features

- Article Name 01 Lorem ipsum dolor sit amet consectetuer adipiscing elit
- Article Name 02 Lorem ipsum dolor sit amet
- Article Name 03 Lorem ipsum

Columns

- Name of Category 01 Lorem ipsum dolor sit amet consectetuer
- Name of Category 02 Lorem ipsum dolor sit amet
- Name of Category 03 Lorem ipsum dolor sit amet consectetuer adipiscing elit.

Past Issues

- Archive Link year/month 01
- Archive Link year/month 02
- Archive Link year/month 03

Right Sidebar: Key BlockQuotes, links, adds other items.

main navigation

- link 01
- link 02
- link 03

Footer Information

link 01 | link 02 | link 03 | link 04 | link 05

OpenSource Online Magazine is proudly powered by WordPress

Remember: If you don't like how your text looks here, a bunch of graphics, columns, and layout adjustments really won't help. Take your time getting the text to look nice and read-well now. You'll have less edits and tweaks to make after the fact.

The Layout

Let's now start to get this stuff look like our sketch!

You'll notice in our XHTML markup that each of our divs has an id name: the divs that are going to be our three columns are wrapped inside an outer div called container2; the main and the left columns are wrapped in a div called container3; and the entire set of divs, including the header and footer, are wrapped in a main div called container.

This structure is what's going to hold our content together and lets WordPress display semantically with the main content first, yet lets the style allow the left column to show up on the left. This structure also insures that the footer stays at the bottom of the longest column.

In the stylesheet, I've set up my basic CSS positioning like the following:

```
body {
  margin: 0px;
}
#container {
  margin: 0 auto;
  width: 900px;
  border: 1px solid #666666;
  font-family: "Trebuchet MS", Verdana, Arial, Helvetica, sans-serif;
  font-size: 12px;
  line-height:16px;
}
#container2 {
  border: 1px solid #0000ff;
}
#container3 {
  width: 670px;
  float:left;
  border: 1px solid #ff0000;
}
#header {
  border: 1px solid #00ff00;
  width: 930px;
  height: 300px;
  /*background: #666666;url("images/css_cs_header.jpg") no-repeat left
top;*/
}
#content {
  margin:0 10px;
  width: 420px;
  float:left;
```

```css
  border: 1px solid #333333;
}
#sidebarLT {
  margin:0 5px;
  width:200px;
  border: 1px solid #ff9900;
  float:right;
}
#sidebarRT {
  margin:0 10px;
  width: 200px;
  float: right;
  border: 1px solid #0000ff;
}
#top_navlist {
  position: absolute;
  top: 170px;
  width: 900px;
  text-align:right;
  border: 1px solid #003333;
}
#pushbottom{
  clear:both;
}
#footer {
  border: 1px solid #000033;
  height: 85px;
  width: 930px;
}
#footerRight{
  margin: 0 10px 0 10px;
  width:400px;
  float:right;
  border: 1px solid #552200;
}
#footerLeft{
  margin: 0 10px;
  width: 400px;
  float:left;
  border: 1px solid #332200;
}
```

Adding the preceding code to my stylesheet gives me a layout that looks like the
the following:

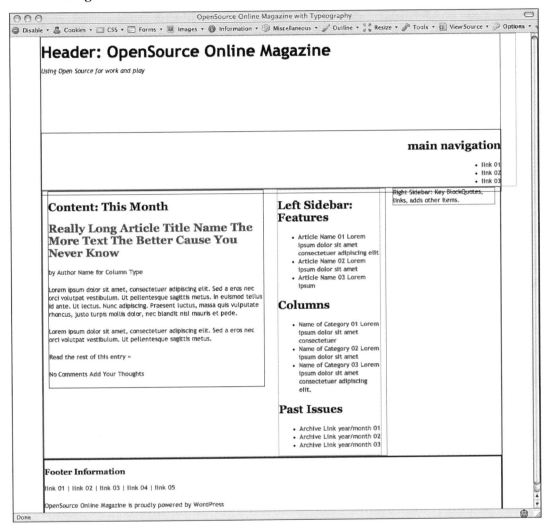

> **Quick CSS layout tip**: As you can see, I like to initially place **bright
> colored** borders in my CSS rules, so I can quickly check (on first glance)
> and see if my widths (or heights) and positioning for each of my divs is
> on target. I tweak from there. As I continue to bring in all the details into
> each CSS rule, I remove these border elements or change them to their
> intended color. You can also use the **Web Developer's Toolbar** to quickly
> see the border area of divs as you drag your mouse over them.

Navigation

As we've discussed, one of the many cool things about WordPress is that it outputs all lists and links with `<li>` tags wrapping each item. This lets you specify if you want the list to be an ordered or unordered list and what id or class you'd like to assign to it, even though by default, all lists are vertical with bullets. Using CSS, you have a wide range of options for styling your WordPress lists. You can turn them into horizontal menus and even multi-level drop down menus! (I'll show you how to create drop-downs and more starting in Chapter 7.)

Awesome CSS List Techniques: **Listamatic** and **Listamatic2** from **maxdesign** (`http://css.maxdesign.com.au/index.htm`) are wonderful resources for referencing and learning different techniques to creatively turn list items into robust navigation devices. It's what I've used to create my Top (Page links nav), Featured, Column, and Past Issues menus in this theme. The Top menu uses **Eric Meyer's tabbed navbar** (`http://css.maxdesign.com.au/listamatic/horizontal05.htm`) and the Sidebar menus use **Eric Meyer's Simple Separators** (`http://css.maxdesign.com.au/listamatic/vertical06.htm`). I just added my own background images and/or colors to these techniques and the navigation came right together.

Time For Action:

I tweaked the code from the two Listamatic sources in a few ways:

1. I added `id="navlist"` to my `ul` inside my `top_navlist` div.
    ```
    <div id="top_navlist">
    <h2>main navigation</h2>
    <ul id="navlist">
    <li><a href="#">link 01</a></li>
    <li><a id="current" href="#">link 02</a></li>
    <li><a href="#">link 03</a></li>
    </ul>
    </div><!--//top_navlist-->
    ```

2. I also hid my h2 headers for the main navigation and footers that I would like people reading my site in-line un-styled to see, but is unnecessary for people viewing the styled site:
    ```
    #top_navlist h2{
        display: none;
    }
    #footer h3{
        display: none;
    }
    ```

3. I massaged the height and width padding on my main li a nav to be about the height and width I imagine my graphical interface images to be.

4. I turned the second list into a class called tocNav, as I intend to apply it to all my blog navigation.

I now have a side bar and top page navigation that looks like the following in the style.css sheet:

```
#top_navlist {
   position: absolute;
   top: 240px;
   width: 900px;
   text-align:right;
   border: 1px solid #003333;
}

#top_navlist h2{
   display: none;
}

#navlist{
   padding: 10px 10px;
   margin-left: 0;
   border-bottom: 1px solid #778;
   font-weight: bold;
}

#navlist li{
   list-style: none;
   margin: 0;
   display: inline;
}

#navlist li a{
   padding: 11px 30px;
   margin-left: 3px;
   border: 1px solid #778;
   border-bottom: none;
   background: #DDE;
  text-decoration: none;
}

#navlist li a:link { color: #448; }
#navlist li a:visited { color: #667; }
```

```
#navlist li a:hover{
  color: #000;
  background: #AAE;
  border-color: #227;
}

#navlist li a#current{
  background: white;
  border-bottom: 1px solid white;
}

/*TOC Nav*/
.tocNav{
  padding-left: 0;
  margin-left: 0;
  border-bottom: 1px solid gray;
  width: 200px;
}

tocNav li{
  list-style: none;
  margin: 0;
  padding: 0.25em;
  border-top: 1px solid gray;
}

tocNav li a { text-decoration: none; }
```

More Navigation–WordPress Specific Styles (OK, Style)

WordPress *does* output a single predefined CSS style. There is a template tag (wp_list_pages) that not only outputs the page links wrapped in an <li> tag, but **adds** the class attribute of page_item to it. If the selected page link *also* happens to be the current page displayed, then an **additional** class called current_page_item is additionally applied.

If your WordPress theme were to take advantage of creating a robust menu for the page links, you could write individual styles for page_item and current_page_item in order to have complete control over your page links menu, including ensuring that your menu displays whichever page is currently active.

Multiple class styles assigned to the same XHTML object tag?! Yep, as you can see in the DOM Source of Selection graphic, you can have as many classes as you want assigned to an XHTML object tag. Simply separate the class names with a blank space and they'll affect your XHTML object in the order that you assign them. Keep in mind the rules of *cascading* apply, so if your second CSS rule has properties in it that match the first, the first rule properties will be overwritten by the second. There are more suggestions for this trick in Chapter 9.

This means we simply change our Listamatic CSS from an id (`#current`) within an `a:href` item, to a class within our `li` item (`current_page_item`) as follows:

```
#navlist li.current_page_item a{
   background: white;
   border-bottom: 1px solid white;
}
```

We now have a page layout that looks like the following:

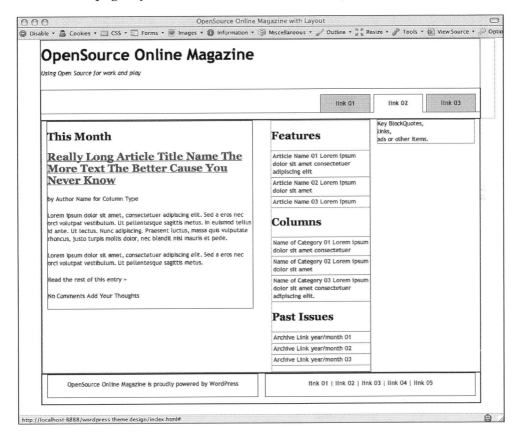

Color Schemes

Now that the general layout is hammered down, we're ready to move onto more exciting design elements.

You'll want a predefined palette of **three to ten** colors arranged in a hierarchy from most prominent to least. I like to create a simple text file which lists the colors' hex values and then add my own comments for each color and how I plan to use it in the theme. This makes it easy for me to add the colors to my CSS file and then later to my Photoshop document as I create graphic interface elements.

 How many colors should I use? I've seen designers do well with a scheme of only three colors, however, six to ten colors is probably more realistic for your design. Keep in mind, WordPress will automatically generate several types of links you'll need to deal with, which will probably push your color scheme out.

Color schemes are the hardest thing to start pulling together. Designers who have years of color theory under their belt still dread coming up with the eye-catching color palettes. But the fact is, color is the first thing people will notice about your site and it's the first thing that will help them *not* notice that it is just another WordPress site (especially if you're taking the 'Simplicity' route and modifying an existing theme).

Two-Minute Color Schemes

When it comes to color schemes, I say, don't sweat it. Mother nature, or at the very least, someone else, already created some of the best color schemes for us. Sure, you can just look at another site or blog you like and see how they handled their color scheme, but it's hard to look at someone else's design and *not* be influenced by more than just their color scheme.

For those intent on an original design, here's my color scheme trick: If your site will be displaying a prominent, permanent graphic or picture (most likely in the header image), start with that. If not, go through your digital photos or peruse a stock photography site and just look for pictures which appeal to you most.

Look through the photos quickly. The smaller the thumbnails the better, content is irrelevant! Just let the photo's color *hit* you. Notice what you like and don't like (or what your client will like, or what suits the project best, etc.), strictly in terms of color.

Color Schemes with Photoshop

Pick one or two images which strike you and drop them into Photoshop. A thumbnail is fine in a pinch, but you'll probably want an image a bit bigger than the thumbnail. Don't use photos with a watermark as the watermark will affect the palette output.

Lose the watermark: Most stock sites have a watermark and there's nothing you can do about that. You can create a free login on gettyimages's photodisc (`http://Photodisc.com`). Once logged in, the watermark is removed from the comp images preview which is about 510 pixels by 330 pixels at 72dpi, perfect for sampling a color palette.

The watermark free image is for reference and mockups only. We won't be using the actual images, just sampling our color palettes from them. If you do end up wanting to use one of these images in your site design or for any project, you must purchase the royalty free rights (royalty free means once you buy them, you can use them over and over wherever you want) or purchase and follow the licensing terms provided by gettyimages's LTD for **rights-managed** images. (Rights-managed images usually have restrictions on where you can use the image, how long it can be on a website, and/or how many prints you can make of the image.)

Once you have an image with colors you like, opened up in Photoshop, go to **Filter | Pixelate | Moziac** and use the filter to render the image into huge pixels. The larger the cell size, the fewer colors you have to deal with, but unfortunately, the more muted the colors become.

I find that a cell size of 50 to 100 for a 72 dpi web image is sufficient (you might need a larger cell size if your photo is of high-resolution). It will give you a nice, deep color range and yet, few enough swatches to easily pick five to ten for your site's color scheme. The best part, if you liked the image in the first place, then any of these color swatches will go together and look great! Instant color scheme!

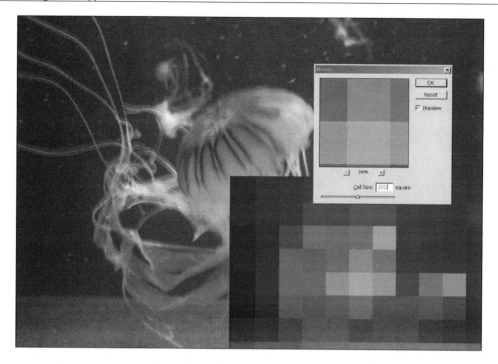

Once the image has been treated with the mosaic filter, just pick up the eyedropper to select your favorite colors. Double-clicking the foreground palette in the tool bar will open up a dialog box and you'll be able to 'copy and paste' the hex number from there into your text file.

Keep track of this text file! Again, it will come in handy when you're ready to paste items into your `style.css` sheet and create graphic interface elements in Photoshop.

```
wordpress_color_theme.txt

light-grey-blue: .#8BA8BA - background & highlights

med-tan .#9E9C76: - some headers

light-tan .#C5BBA0 - highlights

dark-blue .#253A59 - some headers

white .#FFFFFF - text background

dark-reddish .#784B2C - links

light-reddish .#9E745E - link hovers

blue-green .#527382 - some highlights

black .#000000 - text
```

Adding Color to Your CSS

After some thought, I've gone through my CSS sheet and added some color to the existing classes. I either used the `color:` property to change the color of fonts, and even though I'll probably be adding background images to enhance my design, I've gone ahead and also used the `background-color:` property to add color to the backgrounds of `div`s in my layout that are similar to the base color of the background image I'll probably be designing.

The benefits of using the `background-color` property, even though you intend to create images for your design are:

1. In the event your images *happen* to load slowly (due to server performance, not because they're too big), people will see CSS color that is close to the image and the layout won't seem empty or broken.

2. If you can't finish designing images for every detail, sometimes the background color is enough to take the site live and still have it look pretty good. You can always go back in and improve it later.

I've also created **four** new classes to handle my 'TOC section headers' uniquely from regular `h2` headers:

```
.thisMonth{
margin-top: 0;
height: 56px;
line-height: 85px;
background-color: #9E745E;
font-size: 42px;
font-weight: normal;
color: #ffffff;
}
.features{
margin-top: 0;
height: 46px;
line-height: 70px;
background-color: #9E9C76;
font-size: 36px;
font-weight: normal;
color: #ffffff;
}
.columns{
margin-top: 0;
height: 46px;
line-height: 70px;
background-color: #253A59;
font-size: 36px;
font-weight: normal;
```

```
  color: #ffffff;
}
.pastIssues{
margin-top: 0;
font-family: Georgia, Times, serif;
font-size: 31px;
font-weight: normal;
color: #305669;
}
```

Create the Graphical Elements

Now, except for those multi-colored borders I've put around each of my containing divs (they will be removed shortly), I have an XHTML and CSS design that's not half bad. Let's polish it off!

Snap a screenshot (*Ctrl+Prt Scr* on a PC, or use Grab, the free capture program on a Mac) of your layout and paste it into a blank Photoshop document, or open it up into Photoshop.

This is where (after realizing that blocking out layout directly in CSS isn't so bad) I've had web designers argue with me about this 'Rapid Design Comping' process. All your text is now an un-editable graphic and trapped on one opaque layer. Any graphics you place on top of it will obscure the text underneath it, and any graphics you place underneath it, well, can't be seen at all!

So? We're in Photoshop, the program that edits graphic images so well? Keeping in mind that images in your theme design will need to be added using CSS `background-image` techniques, it will probably be best to have your interface graphics set up *behind* your text layer.

Simply use the `Select>Color Range` tool to select and knock out the blocks of color you want replaced with background images in your CSS. A tolerance setting of **32** is more than enough to grab the entire blocks of color. Sure, there are probably places where you plan to replace the text entirely with a graphic, in which case, you can apply the graphic over that area.

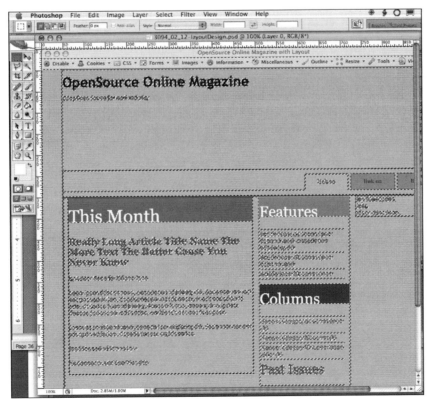

But what if your client makes a change to the text stylings? Easy! Make the requested change to your CSS file, take another screenshot of the updated `index.html` page in your browser and place it back inside your Photoshop file. Yes, you'll have to again knock out some of the blocks of colors so that your graphic interface elements can be seen again. Does making two mouse selections to accomplish that take more time than finding *all* the layers of relevant text and making the style change?

At best, it might be close. But, don't forget the real perk: Your design comp is more than half way ready for production (a.k.a. turning into a working WordPress theme). If the whole mockup was done in Photoshop, you'd still have all the XHTML and CSS creation to go through and then hope you can recreate what's in your Photoshop design comp across browsers.

What about designing in a vector program? If you really love Illustrator or Inkscape so much, you can do one of the two things: One, just design over your text image layer, and if you really must show a comp to a client, add a little text back over the areas obscured by your graphic. Or, you can open the image into Photoshop or GIMP and just as I suggested earlier, use the **Select | Color Range** tool to knock out the main block colors that will be replaced with graphics. Save as a transparent GIF or PNG and import into your vector editor and proceed as suggested above, on layers underneath the text.

Relax and Have Fun Designing

Now that I have my layout set up in Photoshop with the white knocked out, I can proceed with designing my graphic interface elements in the layers underneath.

As you work in your graphic editor, you may come across items that need updating in the CSS to accommodate the interface elements you're designing. I usually deal with these in two ways:

1. If the CSS properties I'm dealing with need to *change in size* (say for instance, I wanted the `top_navigation` tabs to be taller, or I might decide the padding around the WordPress items inside the `sidebarLT div` to be taller or wider to accommodate a graphic), then, as described above, I would make the change in my CSS stylesheet and *take another screenshot* to work with.

2. If the CSS property is just being removed or handled in a way that doesn't change the size, such as borders and display text, I don't take another screenshot. I just edit them out of the PSD layout and make a mental note or production to-do list item to remove the CSS property. Properties that need removing or setting to `display: none` are pretty obvious and easy to take care of while you insert your graphic element images into CSS as `background-image` properties.

There are a couple of 'special needs' cases in my theme design idea that I've been attempting to handle from the start. You may have noticed in my CSS layout that the header is wider at about 930px than my layout at 900px, and it hangs out to the left. I'm going to add a little hint of shadow and that's the amount I've allowed for it.

The border properties I've set up for my main layout elements will help me layout my graphic elements, and as the elements become finalized, I just take the eraser tool or use **Select | Color Range** again to remove them (good thing I made each div border property a different color!).

You can see our final result once we erase the lines and text that will be set to `display:none` or `text-aliged` out of the way:

Slice and Export

When getting ready to slice your images for export, keep in mind that via the background properties in CSS you can control the top, bottom, left, or right placement, x and y repetition, as well as make the image non-repeating. You can also set the background image to 'fixed', and it will not move with the rest of your page if it scrolls.

You'll need to look at your design and start thinking in terms of what will be exported as a complete image, and what will be used as a repeating background image. You'll probably find that your header image is the only thing that will be sliced as a whole. Many of your background images should be sliced so that their size is optimized for use as a repeated image.

If you notice that an image can repeat horizontally to get the same effect, then you'll only need to slice a small *vertical* area of the image. Same goes for noticing images that can repeat vertically. You'll only need to slice a small *horizontal* area of the image and set the CSS repeat rule to repeat-x or repeat-y to load in the image.

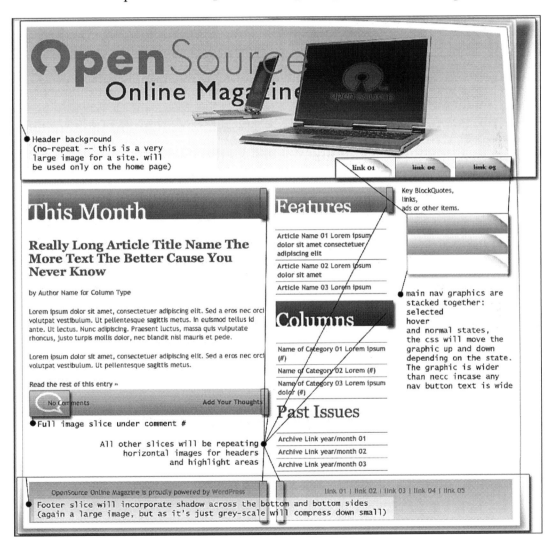

If you'd like more information on how to slice and work with background images, repeating and non-repeating for use with CSS, check out this article from Adobe's site:

http://www.adobe.com/devnet/dreamweaver/articles/
css_bgimages.html

Now that you've placed the slices for each of your theme image elements, export them using the smallest compression options available. Once you have each image, you can import them using the background-image, background-repeat, background-attachment, and background-position CSS properties.

Using CSS 'shorthand' you can handle all of that, including the background-color property via the plain background property, like so:

```
background: #fff url(img.gif) no-repeat fixed 10px 50%;
```

After including our header image, I need to remove the text-header information. Rather than just deleting it from the XHTML page, I set the display for h1, h2, and p to none. That way, people who view the content un-styled will still see appropriate header information. I've also added a #date id so that I can have the current month and year displayed under my magazine text, just like a print magazine.

Here are our #header id rules:

```
#header {
    width: 930px;
    height: 250px;
    background: url("images/oo_mag_header.jpg") no-repeat left top;
}
#header p, #header h1, #header h2/**/ {
    display: none;
}
#header #date{
    position:absolute;
    font-family: Georgia, Times, serif;
    font-size: 16px;
    margin-top: 160px;
    margin-left: 25px;
    color:#253A59;
}
```

And here are our `#top_navlist` id rules, that use a single image rollover technique:

```css
#top_navlist {
  position: absolute;
  top: 260px;
  width: 897px;
  text-align:right;
}
#top_navlist h2{
  display: none;
}
#navlist{
  padding: 10px 10px;
  margin-left: 0;
  border-bottom: 1px solid #ccc;
  font-family: Georgia, Times, serif;
  font-weight: bold;
}
#navlist li{
  list-style: none;
  margin: 0;
  display: inline;
}
#navlist li a{
  padding: 11px 30px;
  margin-left: 3px;
  border: none;
  border-left: 1px solid #ccc;
  background: #8BA8BA url(images/oo_mag_main_nav.jpg)
                              no-repeat top right;
  text-decoration: none;
  color: #253A59;
}
#navlist li a:hover{
  background-color: #9E9C76;
  background-position: right -37px;
  border-color: #C5BBA0;
  color: #784B2C;
  text-decoration: underline;
}
#navlist li.current_page_item a{
  border-bottom: 1px solid white;
  background-color: #fff;
  background-position: right -74px;
}
#navlist li a:visited { color: #253A59; }
```

Wellstyled.com has an excellent tutorial on how to use a single image technique to handle image background rollovers with CSS (`http://wellstyled.com/CSS-nopreload-rollovers.html`).

To see the full and final CSS mockup `style.css` and `index.html` page, please refer to the code download section in the Preface.

The final theme mockup looks like the following in our Firefox browser:

Yes, the final XHTML/CSS mockup is very similar to the Photoshop mockup. It should be almost perfect! You may still notice some slight differences. As I was putting the images into CSS, I discovered that I rather liked having each gradient section outlined using the same base color of the gradient, so I just left some border properties in the stylesheet and changed their color.

I also tested out my `top_navigation` rollover images by adding an extra link (not sure the WordPress site will have a need for a reference page, but if it ever needs it, it can have as many links as can fit across the top there!) and some plausible text to make sure the link area expands with the extra text.

Summary

You have now learned the key theme design considerations to make when planning a WordPress theme. We've also created a great XHTML/CSS mockup. Let's dive right in to cutting it up into a fully working WordPress theme!

3
Coding It Up

We're now going to take our XHTML/CSS mockup and start working it into our WordPress Theme. We'll take a look at how the mockup will be broken apart into template files and how to incorporate WordPress specific PHP code into the template pages to create our working theme.

Got WordPress?

First things first! If by some chance you skipped over Chapter 1 and/or just don't have one yet, you'll need an installation of WordPress to work with. As I explained in Chapter 1, I assume you're familiar with WordPress and its Administration Panel basics and have a development sandbox installation to work with.

> **Sandbox?** I recommend you use the same WordPress version, plug-ins, and widgets that the main project will be using, but don't use the 'live sites' installation of WordPress. Using a development installation (also called 'the sandbox') allows you to experiment and play with your theme creation freely while the main project is free to get started using a built-in default theme to display content. You then also don't have to worry about displaying anything 'broken' or 'ugly' on the live site while you're testing your theme design.

Many hosting providers offer WordPress as an easy 'one-click-install.' Be sure to check with them about setting up an installation of WordPress on your domain.

If you need help getting your WordPress installation up and running, or need an overview of how to use the WordPress Administration Panel, I highly recommend you read Packt Publishing's *WordPress Complete* by Hasin Hayder.

Want to work locally? I spend a lot of time on my laptop, traveling often without a WiFi 'hot spot' in sight. Having a local install of WordPress comes in very handy for theme development. You can install local running versions of PHP5, Apache, and MySQL onto your machine, and afterward, install WordPress 2.

PC users: WAMP Sever2 is a great way to go. Download it from `http://www.wampserver.com/en/`. You can follow 'Jeffro2pt0's' instructions for installing WordPress in this two part series on **weblog tools collection** at:

1. `http://weblogtoolscollection.com/archives/2007/12/30/install-wordpress-locally-1-of-2/`

2. `http://weblogtoolscollection.com/archives/2008/01/03/install-wordpress-locally-part-2-of-2/`

Mac users: You can install MAMP for Mac OSX. Download MAMP from `http://www.mamp.info/en/`. You can follow Michael Doig's instructions to install WordPress at `http://michaeldoig.net/4/installing-mamp-and-WordPress.htm`.

Understanding the WordPress Theme

Let's get familiar with the parts of a theme that your mockup will be separated into.

We'll use the default WordPress theme to review the basic parts of a theme that you'll need to think about as you convert your XHTML/CSS mockup into your theme.

Earlier, I explained that the WordPress theme is the *design* of the site and the WordPress generates the *content*. Thus the content and the design were separate. They are, but your theme does need to have the appropriate **WordPress PHP code** placed into it in order for that content to materialize. It helps if the theme is broken down into **template files**, which make it even easier to maintain with less confusion.

The following figure illustrates how the theme's template files contribute to the rendered WordPress page the user sees on the web.

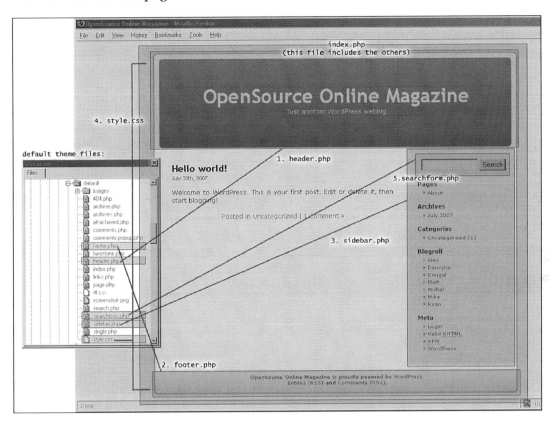

Within a theme, you'll have many individual files called template files. Template files mainly consist of XHTML and PHP code required to structure your site, its content, and functionality.

A WordPress theme's main template files consist of the main index.php file, which uses PHP code to include other template files, such as header.php, footer.php, and sidebar.php. However, as you'll learn throughout this book, you can make as many templates as you feel necessary and configure them any way you want!

Your theme also contains other types of files such as stylesheets (style.css), PHP scripts (like searchform.php), Javascript, and images. All of these elements, together with your template files, make up your complete WordPress theme.

Your WordPress Work Flow

Your work flow will pretty much look like the following:

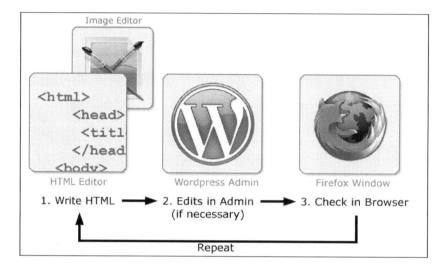

You'll be editing CSS and XHTML in your HTML editor. After each edit, you'll hit **Save**, then use *alt+tab* or task-bar over to your browser window. You'll then hit **Refresh** and check the results (I'll usually direct you *alt+tab*, but however you get to the directed window is fine). Depending on where you are in this process, you might also have two or more browser windows or tabs open—one with your WordPress theme view and others with the key WordPress Administration Panels that you'll be using.

Whether you're using Dreamweaver, or a robust text editor like Coda or HTML-kit, all three of these editors let you FTP directly via a site panel and/or set up a working directory panel (if you're working locally on your own server). **Be sure to use this built-in FTP feature**. It will let you edit and save to the actual theme template files and stylesheet without having to stop and copy to your working directory or upload your file with a standalone FTP client. You'll then be able to use *alt+tab* to move to a browser and view your results instantly after hitting **Save**. Again, this is one of the reasons you're working on a development/sandbox installation of WordPress. You can directly save to the currently selected theme's files and not have to worry about temporarily having something 'ugly' or 'broken' appear on the live site.

Be sure to save regularly and make backups! Backups are sometimes more important than just saving. They enable you to 'roll back' to a previously stable version of your theme design, should you find yourself in a position where your XHTML and CSS has stopped playing nice. Rather than continuing to futz with your code wondering where you broke it, it's sometimes much more cost effective to roll back to your last good stopping point and try again. You can set your preferences in some editors, like HTML-kit, to autosave backups for you in a directory of your choice. However, only you know when you're at a good 'Hey, this is great!' spot. When you get to these points, get in the habit of using the 'Save a Copy' feature to make backups. Your future-futzing-self will love you for it.

Let's Build Our Theme

Have your HTML editor open and set up to display a FTP or local working directory panel so that you have access to your WordPress installation files. Also, have a couple of browser windows open with your WordPress home page loaded into it as well as the WordPress Administration Panel available.

Tabs! Use them. They're one of those neat built-in FireFox features we were talking about. Keep all your WordPress development and admin views in one window. Each tab within a FireFox window is accessible via *Ctrl+1*, *Ctrl+2*, etc. keystrokes. It makes for a much cleaner work space, especially as we'll already be in constant *alt+tab* flip mode. Flipping to the wrong browser windows gets annoying and slows you down. You'll quickly get in the habit of '*Alt+tab, Ctrl+?*' to jump right to your WordPress theme view or administration page, etc.

Tabula Rasa

As I've mentioned in the beginning of this chapter, WordPress separates its themes out into many different template files. As a result, if you want to work on the main body, you'll open up the `index.php` file, but if you want to work on the header layout or DOCTYPE, you'll need to open up the `header.php` file. If you want to deal with the side bar, you'll need to open up `sidebar.php`, and even then, if you want to work on a specific item within the sidebar, you might need to open up *yet another file* such as `searchform.php`.

When you're trying to put your theme together, initially this can be quite overwhelming. My approach to coding up your theme entails the following: (We'll go over each step in detail.)

1. In your new theme directory, create a copy of the existing `index.php` and `style.css` files. Keep these files for reference.

2. Upload your mockup's image directory as well as your `index.html` and `style.css` mockup files to the directory, and rename your `index.html` file to `index.php`.

3. Add WordPress PHP code to your design so that the Word Press content shows up.

4. Once your theme's WordPress content is loading in and your XHTML and CSS still work and look correct, then you can easily pull it apart into your theme's corresponding template files.

5. Once your theme design is separated out into logical template files, you can begin finalizing any special display requirements your theme has, such as a different home page layout, internal page layouts, and extra features.

The other advantage to this approach is that if *any* part of your theme starts to break, you can narrow it down to WordPress PHP code that wasn't copied into its own template file correctly and you have base files to go back to with the clean code (because you've kept the original default theme files, as pointed out in step 1), so you can try again.

Why does WordPress have its theme spread across so many template files? In a nutshell, WordPress does this for powerful flexibility. If your theme design is simple and straightforward enough (that is, you're sure you want all your loops, posts, and pages to look and work *exactly* the same), you can technically just dump everything into a single `index.php` file that contains all the code for the header, footer, sidebar, and plug-in elements. However, as your own theme developing skills progress (and as you'll see with the theme we build in this book), you'll find that breaking the theme apart into individual template files helps you take advantage of the features that WordPress has to offer, which lets you design more robust sites that can easily accommodate many different types of content and layouts.

Time For Action: To get started, we'll create a copy of the existing **default** theme. I'm using a development installation of WordPress on a remote server that I'm FTPing into. If you're working locally, you can follow my instructions using the common desktop commands instead of an FTP client.

1. Inside your WordPress installation, in the `themes` directory (under the `wp-content` directory), locate the `default` theme directory and copy it down locally (or just copy it).

2. Rename the copy of the directory to a theme name which suites your project (and copy it back up to the `themes` directory if working remotely).

3. **Important! Don't skip this step!** WordPress template files follow what's known as the **Template Hierarchy**. Upon renaming the theme directory, open it up. We'll be referencing code from some of the files, but WordPress will use certain files as defaults for different page content if they are left alone. If the theme directory you duplicated has a `home.php` page, a `page.php`, `category.php`, `archive.php`, and/or a `single.php` page, you **must** either remove or rename these files to something else. I usually just rename them to `orig_page.php`, `orig_home.php`, and so on, until I'm ready to incorporate them into my new theme.

 **Find out more about the WordPress Template Hierarchy**: Certain WordPress template pages will override other pages. Not being aware of which files override which ones within your template hierarchy can make troubleshooting your template a real pain. We'll talk about this more in Chapter 6 which deals with *WordPress Reference*, and you can read through the WordPress codex online at `http://codex.wordpress.org/Template_Hierarchy`.

4. After you've made a copy of the `style.css` and the `index.php` files (again, I usually rename them as `orig_style.css`, etc.), upload your mockup's `style.css` and `index.html` sheet (renaming your `index.html` file to `index.php`) into the directory. Now, in your editor, open up the original stylesheet into the Code view. There are eighteen lines of commented out code that contain the theme's information for WordPress. Copy those eighteen lines over into the top of your `style.css` sheet before your style rules. Leaving the text before the colons in each line alone, update the information to the right of each colon to accommodate your own theme. For instance:

```
/*Theme Name: 1 OpenSource Online Magazine
  Theme URI: http://wpdev.eternalurbanyouth.com/
  Description: A WordPress Theme created originally for <a
  href="http://insideopenoffice.org">InsideOpenOffice.org</a> and
  then modified for Packt Publishing's WordPress Theme Design.
  Version: 1.3
  Author: Tessa Blakeley Silver
  Author URI: http://hyper3media.com
  The CSS, XHTML and design is released under GPL:
  http://www.opensource.org/licenses/gpl-license.php
*/
```

5. In your WordPress go to **Administration | Design | Themes (or Administration | Presentation | Themes in 2.3).** There, you'll be able to select the new theme you just duplicated and renamed. (Look carefully! The image is still the **same** as the default theme.)

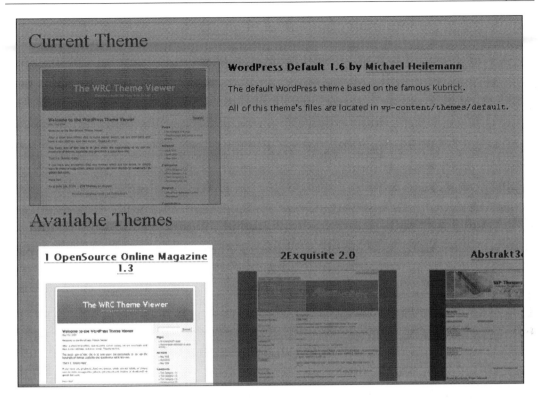

Finding your new theme:

I gave my theme a name that started with '1'. I did this only for development purposes, so it would be easy to find in the list of many themes that come with my installation of WordPress. Before I actually deploy the theme, I'll remove the '1' from the name in the stylesheet. You may do the same when you develop, or you may chose to *intentionally* name your theme with a number or the letter 'A' so that it shows up closer to the top within the list of themes.

Including WordPress Content

When you point your browser to your WordPress Installation, you should see your mockup's unstyled XHTML.

To get your index.php page to read your style.css page, you must replace the @ import url code in your home.php page with the following:

```
<style type="text/css" media="screen">
    @import url("<?php bloginfo('stylesheet_url'); ?>");
</style>
```

Congratulations! That's your first bit of WordPress code. You should now see your styled mockup when you point your browser at your WordPress installation.

We're now ready to start adding WordPress theme code.

The Loop

The next (and I'd say, the most important) bit of WordPress code that I like to tuck into my mockup file is called 'The Loop'. The Loop is an *essential* part of your WordPress theme. It displays your posts in chronological order and lets you define display properties with other PHP bits of code wrapped in XHTML markup.

If by some chance you have no posts to show, the default is to display WordPress' searchform.php file.

Unfamiliar with the Loop? 'The Loop' is one of those core pieces of WordPress PHP code you should brush up on. Understanding how 'The Loop' works in WordPress is incredibly helpful in letting you achieve any special requirements or effects of a custom professional template. To find out more about The Loop, its uses in the main index page, other template pages, and how to customize it, check out the following links on WordPress.org's codex site:

http://codex.wordpress.org/The_Loop_in_Action

http://codex.wordpress.org/The_Loop

I'll start by pasting the following code (which I've copied from the default theme's index.php loop) into my widest column under my **This Month:** header, overwriting the sample content. This code will ensure that the sample posts I've added to my WordPress installation will show up.

```
<?php if (have_posts()) : ?>
    <?php while (have_posts()) : the_post(); ?>
        <div class="post" id="post-<?php the_ID(); ?>">
            <h2><a href="<?php the_permalink() ?>" rel="bookmark"
            title="Permanent Link to <?php the_title(); ?>"><?php
            the_title(); ?></a></h2>
            <small><?php the_time('F jS, Y') ?> <!-- by <?php
            the_author() ?> --></small>
            <div class="entry">
                <?php the_content('<br>Read the rest of this entry
                &raquo;'); ?>
            </div>
            <p class="postmetadata">Posted in <?php the_category(', ')
            ?> | <?php edit_post_link('Edit', '', ' | '); ?>  <?php
            comments_popup_link('No Comments &#187;', '1 Comment
            &#187;', '% Comments &#187;'); ?></p>
```

```
    </div>
<?php endwhile; ?>
<div class="navigation">
    <div class="alignleft"><?php next_posts_link('&laquo; Previous
    Entries') ?></div>
        <div class="alignright"><?php previous_posts_link('Next
        Entries &raquo;') ?></div>
    </div>
<?php else : ?>
    <h2 class="center">Not Found</h2>
    <p class="center">Sorry, but you are looking for something
    that isn't here.</p>
    <?php include (TEMPLATEPATH . "/searchform.php"); ?>
<?php endif; ?>
```

Upon reloading my page, I discover it works just fine and my five sample posts are indeed showing up. However, there's a bit of tweaking to be done:

Keeping in mind that I don't want this theme to be an average blog, and I'm going to continue to emulate my magazine-style concept: The first thing I notice about this loop is that it best suits the standard blog posts. It displays the date, and although commented out, it displays the author. It also lists a **Posted in:** for the **Category** and **Comments** link.

Just like any good magazine, I want to let the content loaded into this theme hang around while the month on the cover is current, and peruse its contents at my leisure. I'm concerned that leaving the full time stamp for each post will encourage some people to not read the content if it happens to be seven days old already or anything like that.

Hence, I'm going to remove the individual time stamp:

```
<?php the_time('F jS, Y') ?>
```

I do want the author's name to show up, but again, more like an article, I think it should be their full name, not their user id or nickname, and the author's name should appear below the post's title with a 'by Author Name'. So, that will have to be uncommented and tweaked to display the author's name. I'll also change the XHTML a bit with and add a new CSS class reference. My author code then changes from `<!--<?php the_author() ?>-->` to the following:

```
<p class="authorName">by <?php the_author_firstname(); ?> <?php the_
author_lastname(); ?> for <?php the_category(', ') ?></p>
```

 I also moved up the category template tag into the paragraph markup and added my own custom class `authorName`.

Because this is the web and not a paper magazine, there are WordPress features I should take advantage of. I feel I want to show what 'Column' (a.k.a. WordPress category) the article has been posted to. I also want to take advantage of having people's comments and ideas expand on the article and help keep it fresh. So, I'll show how many comments have been added to the post. But again, some editing will need to happen as I don't want those two items lumped together at the end of the article section. I've already moved my category template tag up next to my author name display, so what I'm left with is this:

```
<div class="comments"> <div class='commentIcon'><?php comments_
number('No Comments','<span class="bigNum">1</span> response','<span
class="bigNum">%</span> Comments'); ?></div> <?comments_popup_
link('Add Your Thoughts', 'Add Your Thoughts', 'Add Your Thoughts');
?></div>
```

You'll see in the preceding code that I've changed the comments_popup_link template tag to always display Add Your Thoughts and added the comment_number template tag to track how many comments are made on an article. I've also again added my own custom classes called comments, commentsIcon, and bigNum to the markup and changed it from a paragraph tag to a div tag. (So my 'left' and 'right' float assignments would work within it.)

Even though I had most of these text elements handled in my mockup, I'm now seeing what's available to me via the WordPress template tags. You've probably noticed that the classes authorName and bigNum were not the part of my original mockup. I've decided to add them in as I'm developing the WordPress theme. I thought that making the author's name just a little smaller would offset it nicely form the article, and as I created the comment icon, it would be cool, if there were comments, to show them in a big number floating in the middle of the icon.

You will probably come across little details like these yourself, feel free to add them in as you see fit. As long as your changes don't drastically change the layout, your client will not mind. If you think they will, it might be best to add to your original mockup and send a screenshot to the client for approval before proceeding.

Within The Loop (Template Tags): Once you get to rummaging around in your loop (or loops, if you create custom ones for other template pages), you'll quickly see that the default theme's template tags are a bit limiting. There are thousands of custom template tags you can call and reference within the loop (and outside of it) to display the WordPress content. Check out the following link to find out what template tags are available:

http://codex.wordpress.org/Template_Tags

After considering the above discussion, I've come up with a main loop that looks something like the following:

```
<!--//start content loop-->
<?php if (have_posts()) : ?>
    <?php while (have_posts()) : the_post(); ?>
        <div class="post" id="post-<?php the_ID(); ?>">
            <h2><a href="<?php the_permalink() ?>" rel="bookmark"
            title="Permanent Link to <?php the_title(); ?>"><?php
            the_title(); ?></a></h2>
            <p class="authorName">by <?php the_author_firstname(); ?>
            <?php the_author_lastname(); ?> for <?php the_category(',
            ') ?></p>
            <div class="entry">
                <?php the_content('<br>Read the rest of this entry
                &raquo;'); ?>
            </div>
```

```
        <div class="comments"> <div class='commentIcon'><?php
        comments_number('No Comments','<span
        class="bigNum">1</span> response','<span
        class="bigNum">%</span> Comments'); ?></div>
        <?comments_popup_link('Add Your Thoughts', 'Add Your
        Thoughts', 'Add Your Thoughts'); ?></div>
    </div>
<?php endwhile; ?>
    <div class="navigation">
        <div class="alignleft"><?php next_posts_link('&laquo;
        Previous Entries') ?></div>
        <div class="alignright"><?php previous_posts_link('Next
        Entries &raquo;') ?></div>
    </div>
<?php else : ?>
    <h2 class="center">Not Found</h2>
    <p class="center">Sorry, but you are looking for something
    that isn't here.</p>
    <?php include (TEMPLATEPATH . "/searchform.php"); ?>
<?php endif; ?>
<!--//end content loop-->
```

It displays a comment post that looks like this:

The Sidebar

The default theme's `sidebar.php` file displays the following information:

- **Static Page Links**: This is a list of your static pages (content you add via the **Administration | Write | Write Page** tab in the administrator panel as opposed to the **Administration | Write | Write Post** panel. This list is displayed using the `wp_list_pages` template tag.

- **Archive Links**: Again, controlled by a template tag, `wp_get_archives`, this is set to the `type=monthly` default.

- **Category Links** (with how many posts per category): This displays your categories using the `wp_list_categories` template tag.
- **A BlogRoll set of links**: This list is controlled by the `wp_list_bookmarks()` template tag which displays bookmarks found in the **Administration | Blogroll | Manage Blogroll** panel.
- **A set of 'Meta' links** (links to info about the site): These links are hand-coded into the `sidebar.php` page in the default template.

```
                          [Search]

Pages
  » About

Archives
  » September 2007
  » July 2007

Categories
  » Features (3)
  » Office Productivity (1)
  » Uncategorized (1)

Blogroll
  » Alex
  » Donncha
  » Dougal
  » Matt
  » Michel
  » Mike
  » Ryan

Meta
  » Site Admin
  » Logout
  » Valid XHTML
  » XFN
  » WordPress
```

Generally, the above works out great for a more 'standard' blog. But as discussed, I would like my page links to display horizontally up top of my sidebar, and I want my theme to display a vertical sidebar that looks more like the contents page of a magazine.

Time For Action:

1. To start, I'll be treating my archives as **Past Issues**. So showing the month and year will be just fine. Under my **Past Issues** heading I'll add the following code which will display my archive links wrapped in unordered list elements:

```
<!--//start archive list-->
<ul class="tocNav">
   <?php wp_get_archives('type=monthly'); ?>
</ul>
<!--//end archive list-->
```

> **Formatting tip**: You'll see I've wrapped each bit of PHP and its template tag in `<ul class="...">` (unordered list XHTML markup). WordPress will automatically return each item wrapped in `<li>` (list item tags). Adding the unordered list tags (or `<ol>` ordered list tags if you want.) ensures I have a valid list that is easy for me to customize with my CSS.
>
> **XHTML comments**: You'll also note that I'm wrapping most of my WordPress code in `<!--//-->` XHTML comment tags. I do this so that scanning the markup is easier for myself and any other developer who comes across the code (a nice idea for those of you who are looking forward to creating commercial themes to make a little money; the more clear your markup, the less time you'll spend helping purchasers troubleshoot your theme). Also, indicating where WordPress code starts and ends as well as what kind of code it is, will also come in very handy when we get ready to break the code out into template pages, reducing the chance of possible cut-and-paste errors that can occur.

2. Next, my **Columns** are really just a list of my categories. The default sidebar lists the title as **Categories,** but as I have my own special header hand-coded into the side bar, I've removed the following:

```
&title_li=<h2>Categories</h2>
```

I have changed it to this:

```
&title_li=
```

It gives me the code under my **Columns** header that looks like this:

```
<!--//start categories list-->
<ul class="tocNav">
   <?php wp_list_categories('show_count=1&title_li='); ?>
</ul>
<!--//end categories list-->
```

3. Next, my **Features** will require a little bit of finessing. I would like WordPress to display the most recent five posts that are only in the **Features** category. There are a few clean template tags that will display the most recent post titles, but they don't seem to let me limit the posts to just coming from my **Features** category.

Because I understand a little PHP, I'll include a small custom loop which will use three WordPress template tags to call in the post information for the last five posts in category **3** (which is my **Features** category), then just display the perma link for each post and its title.

Again, as long as you recognize what the template tags look like and how to paste them into your theme template pages, you don't have to understand PHP or write any special scripts yourself. You can do a whole lot with just the existing template tags.

Understanding PHP and how to craft your own bits of code and loops will enable you to have no limits on your theme's capabilities. The following script has the WordPress template tags highlighted in it, so you can see how they're used.

```
<!--//start recent features list-->
<ul class="tocNav">
    <?php
    global $post;
    $myposts = get_posts('numberposts=5&category=3');
    foreach($myposts as $post):
        setup_postdata($post);?>
        <li><a href="<?php the_permalink() ?>"><?php the_title();
        ?></a></li>
    <?php endforeach; ?>
</ul>
<!--//end recent features list-->
```

Custom Selecting Post Data: You'll probably notice that the setup_postdata(); function isn't listed in WordPress.org's template tag reference page, it's actually a WordPress formatting function. If you're interested in PHP and would like to learn more about being able to infinitely customize WordPress content into your themes, I'll discuss this and some other formatting functions in Chapter 6, it's also worth it to check out the topic on WordPress codex site from http://codex.wordpress.org/Displaying_Posts_Using_a_Custom_Select_Query.

4. Last, I am ready for my page navigation. At the moment, my only static pages are **About** and **Contact**. I'll place the `wp_list_pages` template tag into my `top_navlist` div tags as follows:

```
<!--//start page nav list-->
<ul id="navlist">
    <?php wp_list_pages('title_li=' ); ?>
</ul>
<!--//end page nav list-->
```

Breaking It Up–Separating Your Theme Into Template Files

As I mentioned earlier, the advantage to having your WordPress theme's parts separated into individual template pages is that your theme will be more flexible and able to accommodate a wider range of content. As nice as my theme currently looks, there are some problems with it that can only be dealt with if I break the theme's design up into multiple WordPress template pages.

To start, I only want that huge 300 pixel high header graphic to load on the home page. It's neat to give the feel of a magazine cover, but once the reader has moved onto a full article (a.k.a. post) or one of my static pages, I'd rather not have it there eating up screen real estate that the reader could be using to read more content without having to scroll. Like wise, the **This Month** header only needs to be on the home page, not on any internal page.

Also, while I do want the **Features**, **Columns**, **Past Issues** sidebar navigation to show up in a full article view page, I don't want that navigation sidebar on the **About** and **Contact** static pages. I'll have them click on an additional link in the top nav called **The Zine** to get back to the home page view.

Again, because WordPress is so flexible, it's super easy to add this extra link to the top nav by just adding the list item under the template tag like so:

```
<ul id="navlist">
    <li><a href="/">The Zine</a></li>
    <?php wp_list_pages('title_li=' ); ?>
</ul>
```

That link **The Zine** will now let people go back to the home post page if they view one of my static pages. As my CSS style is targeting list items in the `top_navigation` div, the new list items automatically pick up the same styling as the WP generated items.

Next, the loop needs slightly different formatting between my posts and static pages. Posts are being treated like articles, so I have template tags that announce 'by Author Name for Category Name,' but on the static pages, to have the page title **About** and then 'by Author Name' is a little ridiculous.

Last, I'll need the full article pages to display comments under the article with the 'Add Comments' form underneath that, so if people click on the **Add Your Thoughts** link, they'll be anchor-tagged down to the form for the post.

The Home Page

To ensure that only the home page has the main header and **This Month** show up, I'll take advantage of WordPress' template pages. Along with `index.php`, `header.php`, `footer.php`, and `sidebar.php`, you can also create a template file called `home.php`.

If you have a template file called `home.php`, WordPress will automatically use this as your theme's home page. If WordPress scans your theme's directory and finds no `home.php` page, WordPress will use the `index.php` page as the default.

Many theme developers use a `home.php` page to set up a static home page or 'splash' page for their site. I'll be keeping the loop in mine, but it's the same idea.

Because I don't intend for my theme's blog posts (a.k.a. articles) to have a different URL location from my home page, this method for separating out some visual elements between my *home* page and *internal* pages is just fine.

However, if you do intend to have different URL locations for your blog posts versus the home page (that is `http://myblogurl.com` for the home page and `http://myblogurl.com/blog` for the blog posts page), you should heed WordPress' latest 2.1 suggestion of not naming your homepage as `home.php` and setting your home page up via your **Administration | Options | Reading** panel. Not doing so may mean trouble for your **more** link button. You can find out more on WordPress' site: `http://codex.wordpress.org/Creating_a_Static_Front_Page`.

Time For Action:

1. Because I like the way my `index.php` looks and works strictly as a home page, I'll start off by just duplicating my `index.php` file and renaming it to `home.php` inside my theme's directory. Even though the markup is same, WordPress is now automatically reading from the `home.php` page instead of the `index.php` page. (Making a small, temporary difference in the markup of the `home.php` will prove this if you'd like to test it.)

2. Now that it's done, I know that the **Features**, **Columns**, and **Past Issues** side bar will be used in post pages and the home page, so I'll pull the markup and code from my `#sidebarLT` div and paste it into my `sidebar.php` page. I'll then include that page into my `home.php` page by using the following code:

    `<?php get_sidebar(); ?>`

3. I'll do the same with my footer code, cutting and pasting everything from my footer div into the `footer.php` file using the following code:

    `<?php get_footer(); ?>`

4. I'll test this in the browser, and upon its working, I'll duplicate those included files from my `home.php` page into in my `index.php` page. (It will be handy to have the `includes` in place when we make our internal page.)

> **Extra Credit**: In my `#header` div, I have a div id called `#date`. I want to display the full name for the current month and year. The best route for this is to just apply some basic PHP directly. I enter the following PHP code into my `#date` div:
>
> ```
> <div id="date"><?php echo date("F Y"); ?></div>
> ```

Time For Action: The very last detail I'll include is my third column. I want to be able to manually control the advertisements (be it Google AdSense or AdBright ads) and custom feature graphic links that go in here. No one else should be able to edit this `include` through the WordPress admin panel, so using a little of my own PHP, I'll create a page called `sidebar2.php` which I'll place in my own directory in the root of my WordPress installation and manually include this page with a standard PHP `include` call, like so:

```php
<?php include(TEMPLATEPATH . '/sidebar2.php'); ?>
```

Including TEMPLATEPATH will point to your current theme directory.

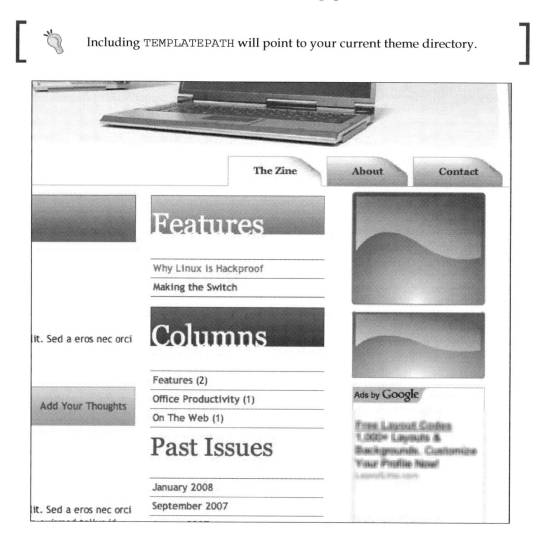

Internal Pages

Now that our home page is working, it's time to modify the index.php file for the internal page layout.

Using the same 'Rapid Prototyping' process we used to generate the home page layout in Chapter 2, I've also created a mockup of my internal layout (the internal layout is included with the home page layout in the zip file, available for download at http://packtpub.com/?/?tbd).

Time For Action:

The biggest difference between my internal pages and my home page is the header. As a result, it will be easier to start off by just copying my current home.php page back over into the index.php page.

1. I'll rename the #header div id and give it a different id called #intHeader and create a new style that calls in my thinner, internal page header graphic and sets the height of the div accordingly.

2. Next, I'll remove the <h2> header that displays **This Month:**. I'll also create a div id rule for the header's #date and create a style for that which will move my magazine's PHP date code to the top-right of my internal header.

3. Next, my top_navigation id will have to change to intTop_navlist, and I'll amend the top_navlist rules that control the unordered list.

4. Now, I just need to add the 'Comments' display and 'Add Comments' form to my index page. I'll do so by placing the following code at the end of my loop in the index.php page, under the the_content template tag like so:

```
...<div class="entry">
  <?php the_content('<br>Read the rest of this entry &raquo;');
  ?>
</div>
    <div id="pagecomments">
    <?php comments_template(); ?>
    </div>
  <p class="articleComment">
```

5. This will pull in the default theme's comments.php page, which works quite well for my purpose. It just requires that I create a few additional style elements for the input box and the submit button so that it works well with my theme.

6. I'll now just break the header div out of my index.php page and copy it into a header.php file in my theme's directory. Then in index.php, I'll call in the header block with:

```
<?php get_header(); ?>
```

This gives us an internal page that looks like this:

Static Pages

Static pages are the pages you generate in WordPress using the **Write (or Manage) | Pages** instead of **Write (or Manage) | Posts**. Our index.php page now effectively handles all the secondary requests. This is great, except my static **About** and **Contact** pages don't need the comment posted or #sidebarLT information to to be displayed. This is where another one of those great WordPress template files comes in—the page.php template file.

Time For Action:

Create a `page.php` file and paste your `index.php` information into it.

The first quick and easy thing we can do is remove the `class="current_page_item"` from **The Zine** link we've added on to our page display.

1. You can now remove the WordPress' `comments_template` template tag and XHTML markup from the loop:

```
<div id="pagecomments">
   <?php comments_template(); ?>
</div>
```

You can also remove the number of comments code and the **Add Your Thoughts** code from the loop:

```
<div class="comments"> <div class='commentIcon'><?php comments_
number('No Comments','<span class="bigNum">1</span> response','<span
class="bigNum">%</span> Comments'); ?></div> <?comments_popup_
link('Add Your Thoughts', 'Add Your Thoughts', 'Add Your Thoughts');
?></div>
```

2. You can also completely remove the `#sidebarLT` div now:

```
<div id="sidebarLT">
<?php get_sidebar();?>
</div><!--//sidebarLT  -->
```

3. Without the side column, the content div doesn't have to be restricted to `430px` wide. Change the div id to `pgContent` and add a new CSS rule to your `style.css` page:

```
<!-- Begin #content -->
   <div id="pgContent">...
#pgContent {
 margin:0 0 0 10px;
 width: 650px;
 float:left;
}
```

Quick Recap

OK to recap, you should have three views now:

1. One template view for your home page that shows the large home page header and link to comments.

2. One template view for your article (post) pages, which uses the internal header and displays your comments. Because this layout is for articles, **The Zine** link is left with the class `current_page_item`.

3. And last, one template page view for 'static' pages.

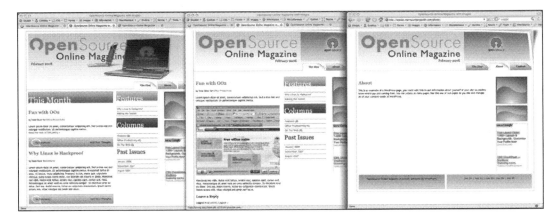

Fun with Other Page Layouts

Because we renamed (or removed) `archive.php` and `category.php` from our template directory, the `index.php` template file is covering links to **Categories** (a.k.a. **Columns**) and archives (a.k.a. **Past Issues**).

This on its own is working well enough, but you can certainly improve these pages by pasting your `index.php` code into a new `archive.php` and/or `category.php` page, and then customize those page views even further.

For instance, you could place the following code into your `category.php` page, just above the loop:

```
<h3>You're reading the: <?php the_category(', ')?> column</h3>
```

It would give you the following result:

Remember, WordPress has a host of template tags to help you add content to any of your template files, be they includes or page views. We'll discuss important WordPress template tags in Chapter 6.

Don't Forget About Your 404 Page

Error 404 pages are where servers direct browsers when a URL seeks a missing page. While it's easy to think you won't really need a 404 page with a WordPress install, you'd be surprised. Even though all the links to the article or page you deleted are removed automatically from within your site, someone else might have created a link on their site to your post, which will no longer work. The 404.php template page is how you'll handle these requests.

You might have noticed, the PHP code we use for the home.php and index.php page loops have a 'catch-all fix' in case posts are not found, which will display a nice message and the search.php template page. The 404.php template page in the default WordPress theme does not do this (and it's also not set up to display our other template files and CSS).

Because the 404.php page does not require the comments or author information display, the template page that is closest to it is our page.php file. However, we want to give people additional options to get back into our content, so we'll want to place the #sidebarLT div back into it.

Time For Action:

1. Copy the contents of your page.php template file into the 404.php template file.

2. You can remove the *entire loop* from the file.

3. Place in some encouraging text and the PHP code to include the search.php template file:

   ```
   <h2 class="center">Not Found</h2>
   <p class="center">Sorry, but you are looking for something that
                                           isn't here.</p>
   <?php include (TEMPLATEPATH . "/searchform.php"); ?>
   ```

4. Add the #sidebarLT XHTML and PHP WordPress template tag back in *under* the content div:

   ```
   <div id="sidebarLT">
   <?php get_sidebar();?>
   </div><!--//sidebarLT  -->
   ```

These steps should give you a 404 error page that looks like this:

Summary

We've now completed the OpenSource Online Magazine WordPress theme. Great Job!

It's probably clear that you can take advantage of all sorts of custom WordPress template hierarchy pages, and endlessly continue to tweak your theme in order to display custom information and layouts for all types of different scenarios.

How much customization your theme requires depends entirely on what you want to use it for. If you know exactly how it's going to be used and you'll be the administrator controlling it, then you can save time by covering the most obvious page displays the site will need to get it rolling and occasionally creating new page view files should the need arise. If you intend to release the theme to the public, then the more customized page views you cover, the better. You never know how someone will want to apply your theme to their site.

You've now learned how to set up your development environment and an HTML editor for a smooth work flow. You now have a theme design that uses semantic, SEO friendly XHTML and CSS, and has been broken down into WordPress template pages for flexibility in your layouts. Believe it or not, we're not quite done!

In the next chapter, we'll continue working with our XHTML and CSS layout, showing you some tips and tricks for getting it to display properly in all the browsers, debugging IE quirks as well as running it through a thorough validation process.

4

Debugging and Validaton

For simplicity's sake, I've made this process a separate chapter. However, as you work on and develop your own WordPress themes, you will no doubt discover that life will go much smoother if you debug and validate at *each step* of your theme development process. The full process will pretty much go like this: Add some code, check to see the page looks good in FireFox, validate, then check it in IE and any other browsers you and your site's audience use, validate *again* if necessary, add the next bit of code... repeat as necessary until your theme is complete.

In this chapter, I'm going to cover the basic techniques of debugging and validation that you should be employing throughout your theme's development. We'll dive into the W3C's XHTML and CSS validation services, and I'll walk you through using FireFox's JavaScript/Error Console for robust debugging, as well as introduce you to the FireBug extension and the Web Developer's Toolbar. I'll also give you a little troubleshooting insight as to some of the most common reasons 'good code goes bad,' especially in IE, and the various ways to remedy the problems.

Don't Forget About Those Other Browsers and Platforms

I'll mostly be talking about working in Firefox and then 'fixing' for IE. This is perhaps, unfairly, assuming you're working on Windows or a Mac and that the source of all your design woes will (of course) be Microsoft IE's fault. But as I mentioned in Chapter 1, this book is *not* about only using Firefox! You must check your theme in *all* browsers and if possible, other platforms, especially the ones you know your audience uses the most.

I surf with Opera a lot and find that sometimes JavaScripts can 'hang' or slow that browser down, so I debug and double-check scripts for that browser. (We'll discuss more on JavaScripts in Chapter 8.) I'm a freelance designer and find a lot of people who are also in the design field use a Mac (like me), and visit my sites using Safari, so I occasionally take advantage of this and write CSS that caters to the Safari browser. (Safari will interpret some neat CSS 3 properties that other browsers don't yet.)

Generally, if you write valid markup and code that looks good in Firefox, it will look good in all the other browsers (including IE). Markup and code that goes awry in IE is usually easy to fix with a work-around.

Firefox is a tool, nothing more! That's the only reason why this book tends to focus on Firefox. Firefox contains features and plug-ins that we'll be taking advantage of to help us streamline the theme development process and aid in the validation and debugging of our theme. Use it just like you use your HTML/code editor or your image editor. When you're not developing, you can use whatever browser you prefer.

Introduction to Debugging

Remember in Chapter 3, our initial work-flow chart?

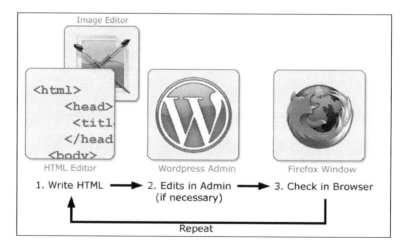

I was insistent that your work-flow pretty much be as *edit -> check it -> then go back and edit some more*. The main purpose of visually checking your theme in FireFox after adding each piece of code is so that you can see if it looks OK, and if not, immediately debug that piece of code. Running a validation check as you work just doubly ensures you're on the right track.

So, your work-flow really ends up looking something more like this:

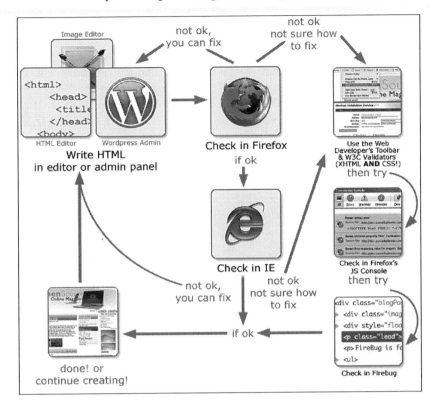

You want to work with nice, small pieces or 'chunks' of code. I tend to define a *chunk* in XHTML markup as no more than one div section, the internal markup, and any WordPress template tags it contains. When working with CSS, I try to only work with one id or class rule at a time. Sometimes, while working with CSS, I'll break this down even further and test after *every* property I add to a rule, until the rule looks as I intend and validates.

As soon as you see something that doesn't look right in your browser, you can check for validation and then fix it. The advantage of this work-flow is you know exactly what needs to be fixed and what XHTML markup or PHP code is to blame. All the code that was looking fine and validating before, you can ignore. The recently added markup and code is also the freshest in your mind, so you're more likely to realize the solution needed to fix the problem.

If you add too many chunks of XHTML markup or several CSS rules before checking it in your browser, then discover something has gone awry, you'll have twice as much sleuthing to do in order to discover which (bit or bits) of markup and code are to blame. Again, your **fail-safe** is your *backup*.

You should be regularly saving backups of your theme at good stable stopping points. If you do discover that you just can't figure out where the issue is, rolling back to your last stable stopping point and starting over might be your best bet to getting back on track.

As mentioned in Chapter 2, you'll primarily design for FireFox and then apply any required fixes, hacks, and workarounds to IE. You can do that for each piece of code you add to your theme. As you can see in the preceding figure, first check your theme in FireFox and if there's a problem, fix it for FireFox first. Then, check it in IE and make any adjustments for that browser.

At this point, you guessed it, more than half of the debugging process will depend directly on your own eyeballs and aesthetics. If it looks the way you intended it to look and works the way you intended it to work, check that the code validates and move on. When one of those three things doesn't happen (it doesn't look right, work right, or validate), you have to stop and figure out why.

Troubleshooting Basics

Suffice to say, it will usually be obvious when something is wrong with your WordPress theme. The most common reasons for things being 'off' are:

- Mis-named, mis-targeted, or inappropriately-sized images.
- Markup text or PHP code that affects or breaks the Document Object Model (DOM) due to being inappropriately placed or having syntax errors in it.
- WordPress PHP code copied over incorrectly, producing PHP error displays in your template, rather than content.
- CSS rules that use incorrect syntax or conflict with later CSS rules.

The first point is pretty obvious when it happens. You see no images, or worse, you might get those little ugly 'x'd' boxes in IE if they're called directly from the WordPress posts or pages. Fortunately, the solution is also obvious: you have to go in and make sure your images are named correctly if you're overwriting standard icons or images from another theme. You also might need to go through your CSS file and make *sure* the relative paths to the images are correct.

For images that are not appearing correctly because they were mis-sized, you can go back to your image editor, fix them, and then re-export them, or you might be able to make adjustments in your CSS file to display a height and/or width that is more appropriate to the image you designed.

Don't forget about casing! If by some chance you happen to be developing your theme with an installation of WordPress on a local Windows machine, do be careful with the upper and lower casing in your links and image paths. Chances are, the WordPress installation that your theme is going to be installed into is more likely to be on a Unix or Linux web server. For some darn reason, Windows (even if you're running Apache, not IIS) will let you reference and call files with *only* the correct spelling required. Linux, in addition to spelling, requires the upper and lower casing to be correct. You must be careful to duplicate *exact* casing when naming images that are going to be replaced and/or when referencing your own image names via CSS. Otherwise, it will look fine in your local testing environment, but you'll end up with a pretty ugly theme when you upload it into your client's installation of WordPress for the first time (which is just plain embarrassing).

For the latter two points, one of the best ways to debug syntax errors that cause visual 'wonks' is not to have syntax errors in the first place (don't roll your eyes just yet).

This is why, in the last figure of our expanded work-flow chart, we advocate you to *not only* visually check your design as it progresses in FireFox and IE, but also *test for validation*.

Why Validate?

Hey, I understand it's easy to add some code, run a visual check in FireFox and IE, see everything looks OK, and then flip right back to your HTML editor to add more code. After-all, time is money and you'll just save that validation part until the very end. Besides, validation is just icing on the cake. Right?

The problem with debugging purely based on visual output is, all browsers (some more grievously than others) will try their best to help you out and properly interpret less than ideal markup. One piece of invalid markup might very well look OK initially, until you add more markups and then the browser can't interpret your intentions between the two types of markup anymore. The browser will pick its own best option and display something guaranteed to be ugly.

You'll then go back and futz around with the *last* bit of code you added (because everything was fine until you added that last bit, so that *must* be the offending code) which may or may not fix the problem. The *next* bits of code might create other problems and what's worse that you'll recognize a code chunk that you know should be valid! You're then frustrated, scratching your head as to why the last bit of code you added is making your theme 'wonky' when you know, without a doubt, it's perfectly fine code!

The worst case scenario I tend to see of this type of visual-only debugging is that the theme developers get desperate and start randomly making all sorts of odd hacks and tweaks to their markup and CSS to get it to look right.

Miraculously, they often *do* get it to look right, but in only *one* browser. Most likely, they've inadvertently discovered what the first invalid syntax was and unwittingly applied it across *all* the rest of their markup and CSS. Thus, that one browser started consistently interpreting the *bad* syntax! The theme designer then becomes convinced that the other browser is awful and designing these non-WYSIWYG, dynamic themes is a pain.

Avoid all that frustration! Even if it looks great in both browsers, run the code through the W3C's XHTML and CSS validators. If something turns up invalid, no matter how small or pedantic the validator's suggestion might be (and they do seem pedantic at times), incorporate the suggested fix into your markup *now*, before you continue working. This will keep any small syntax errors from compounding future bits of markup and code into big visual 'uglies' that are hard to track down and troubleshoot.

PHP Template Tags

The next issue you'll most commonly run into is mistakes and typos that are created by 'copying and pasting' your WordPress template tags and other PHP code incorrectly. The most common result you'll get from invalid PHP syntax is a 'Fatal Error.' Fortunately, PHP does a decent job of trying to let you know what file name and line of code in the file the offending syntax lives (yet another reason why in Chapter 3 I highly recommend an HTML editor that lets you view the line number in the **Code** view).

If you get a 'Fatal Error' in your template, your best bet is to open the file name that is listed and go to the line in your editor. Once there, search for missing `<?php ?>` tags. Your template tags should also be followed with parenthesis followed by a semicolon like `();`. If the template tag has parameters passed in it, make sure *each* parameter is surrounded by single quote marks, that is, `template_tag_name('parameter name', 'next_parameter');`.

CSS Quick Fixes

Last, your CSS file might get fairly big, fairly quickly. It's easy to forget you already made a rule and/or just accidentally create another rule of the same name. It's all about cascading, so whatever comes last, overwrites what came first.

> **Double rules**: It's an easy mistake to make, but validating using W3C's CSS validator will point this out right away. However, this is *not* the case for double **properties** within rules! W3C's CSS validator will not point out double properties if both properties use correct syntax. This is one of the reasons why the !important hack returns valid. (We'll discuss this hack just a little further down in this chapter under *To Hack or Not to Hack*.)

Perhaps you found a site that has a nice CSS style or effect you like, and so you copied those CSS rules into your theme's style.css sheet. Just like with XHTML markup or PHP code, it's easy to introduce errors by miscopying the bits of CSS syntax in. A small syntax error in a property towards the bottom of a rule may seem OK at first, but cause problems with properties added to the rule later. This can also affect the entire rule or even the rule after it.

Also, if you're copying CSS, be aware that older sites might be using depreciated CSS properties, which might be technically OK if they're using an older HTML DOCTYPE, but won't be OK for the XHTML DOCTYPE you're using.

Again, validating your markup and CSS as you're developing will alert you to syntax errors, depreciated properties, and duplicate rules which could compound and cause issues in your stylesheet down the line.

Advanced Troubleshooting

Take some time to understand the XHTML hierarchy. You'll start running into validation errors and CSS styling issues if you wrap a 'normal' (also known as a 'block') element inside an 'in-line' only element, such as putting a header tag inside an anchor tag (<a href, <a name, etc.) or wrapping a div tag inside a span tag.

Avoid triggering *quirks mode* in IE! This, if nothing else, is one of the most important reasons for using the W3C HTML validator. There's no real way to tell if IE is running in quirks mode. It doesn't seem to output that information anywhere (that I've found). However, if any part of your page or CSS isn't validating, it's a good way to trigger quirks mode in IE.

The first way to avoid quirks mode is to make sure your DOCTTYPE is valid and correct. If IE doesn't recognize the DOCTYPE (or if you have huge conflicts, like an XHTML DOCTYPE, but then you use all-cap, HTML 4.0 tags in your markup), IE will default into quirks mode and from there on out, who knows what you'll get in IE.

> **My theme stopped centering in IE!** The most obvious thing that happens when IE goes into quirks mode is that IE will stop centering your layout in the window properly if your CSS is using the margin: 0 auto; technique. If this happens, immediately fix all the validation errors in your page. Another big obvious item to note is if your div layers with borders and padding are sized differently between browsers. If IE is running in quirks mode it will incorrectly render the **box model**, which is quite noticeable between FireFox and IE if you're using borders and padding in your divs.

Another item to keep track of is to make sure you don't have *anything* that will generate any text or code **above** your DOCTYPE.

FireFox will read your page until it hits a valid DOCTYPE and then proceed from there, but IE will just break and go into quirks mode.

Fixing CSS Across Browsers

If you've been following our *debug->validate* method described in the chapter, then for all intents and purposes, your layout should look pretty spot-on between *both* the browsers.

Box Model Issues

In the event that there is a visual discrepancy between FireFox and IE, in most cases it's a box model issue arising because you're running in quirks mode in IE. Generally, box model hacks apply to pre IE 6 browsers (IE 5.x) and apply to IE6 if it's running in quirks mode. Again, running in quirks mode is to be preferably avoided, thus eliminating most of these issues. If your markup and CSS are validating (which means you shouldn't be triggering quirks mode in IE, but I've had people 'swear' to me their page validated yet quirks mode was being activated), you might rather 'live with it' than try to sleuth what's causing quirks mode to activate.

Basically, IE 5.x and IE6 quirks mode don't properly interpret the box model standard and thus, 'squish' your borders and padding *inside* your box's width, instead of *adding* to the width as the W3C standard recommends.

However, IE does properly add margins! This means that if you've got a div set to 50 pixels wide, with a 5 pixel border, 5 pixels of padding, and 10 pixels of margin in FireFox, your div is actually going to be 60 pixels wide with 10 pixels of margin around it, taking up a total space of 70 pixels..

In IE quirks mode, your box is kept at 50 pixles wide (meaning it's probably taller than your FireFox div because the text inside is having to wrap at 40 pixels), yet it does have 10 pixels of margin around it. You can quickly see how even a one pixel border, some padding, and a margin can start to make a *big* difference in layout between IE and FireFox!

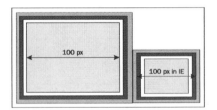

Everything Is Relative

Most Windows users are still predominately using IE 6 (and IE7 is gaining). When it comes to validating and debugging for IE, I find that as long as I stay in strict mode and not fall into quirks mode, I don't have too many issues with box model rendering. Occasionally, I still notice that relative CSS values such as % or .ems render a little differently, but that's not box model, so much as what the two browsers interpret, say, 20% to be in pixels. Even so, as long as your layout doesn't look weird, it's generally OK if your theme's container divs are a hair wider in one browser over the other. If you're using relative values to measure everything out, your placement will stay intact.

> **What are the major browsers?** According to W3schools, at the time of this writing, IE6 and IE7 together make up a little over half of the total users. Firefox comes in second. Use this link to keep up on browsing trends: `http://www.w3schools.com/browsers/browsers_stats.asp`.
>
> As I mentioned at the beginning of this chapter, you still need to look and make sure your site is rendering properly in as many browsers as you have access to. As a bonus, if you have access to multiple platforms (like Linux or Mac, if you're on a PC), it's good to check and see how popular browsers who have distributions for those OSs look on them too.
>
> If you're using valid markup, you'll be pleasantly surprised to find out that your site looks great in all sorts of browsers and platforms. Occasionally, if you run into a situation where something doesn't look right, you can then decide if that browser is critical to your users and if you'd like to fix it.

To Hack or Not to Hack

If for some reason, you feel you know what you're getting into and have intentionally used markup syntax that's triggering quirks mode in IE (or you just can't figure out why, or maybe your client insists on designing for IE5.x for Windows), then it's time for some hacks.

The cleanest hack is the `!important` hack. I like it because it lets CSS still render as valid. However, you should note that the `!important` value is the **valid** syntax and meant to be used as an accessibility feature of CSS. It's *not* a value that was ever meant to affect the design.

The fact that IE does not recognize it is a bug and though it's very simple and easy to implement, it's **not recommended** to be used liberally as a design fix. The understanding is, eventually IE will fix this bug so that it adheres to accessibility standards and then your hack will no longer work (especially if IE doesn't change anything about how it runs in quirks mode).

> **Remember:** *All* CSS hacks rely on exploiting various bugs in IE to some extent and may or may not continue to work with future service patches and upgrades to IE.

To implement the `!important` hack, take the width, height, margin, or padding property that has the discrepancy in it and double it. Place the value that looks best in FireFox *first* and add the `!important` value after it. Then, place the value in the duplicate property that looks best in IE *below* the first property. You should have something that looks like this:

```
.classRule{
    height: 100px !important;
    height: 98px;
}
```

FireFox and all other browsers will read the value with the !important value after it, as if it were the *last* value in the rule. IE ignores the !important value and thus regular-old cascading kicks in, so it reads the actual last property value in the rule.

Other IE hacks include using the star selector bug hack (*) and the _ underscore hack (_). Both hacks work on the same general principle as the !important hack, that IE does or doesn't recognize something that all the other browsers do or don't recognize themselves. You can find out more about the underscore hack from WellStyled. com (http://wellstyled.com/css-underscore-hack.html). A good overview of the star selector bug can be found at Info.com (http://www.info.com.ph/~etan/ w3pantheon/style/starhtmlbug.html).

Be aware, those last two hacks *will show up as validation errors* in your CSS. Plus, the star and underscore hacks are rumored to no longer be viable in IE7 (ah! fixing those bugs!). You must choose to use these three hacks at your discretion.

Out-of-the-Box-Model Thinking

Your best bet is again to not use hacks. This is achieved in a couple of ways. First, you can break your XHTML markup down a little more. That means, for example, instead of one div layer:

```
<div id="leftSide">...</div>
```

...with the assigned rule:

```
#leftSide{
width: 200px;
border: 2px;
padding: 10px;
}
```

... which is clearly going to give you problems in quirks mode IE, because the div will stay at 200 pixels wide and 'squish' your border and padding inside it, it would be better to tuck an extra div or other XHTML element *inside* the leftSide id like so:

```
<div id="leftSide"><div>...</div></div>
```

Then, you can control the width and borders much more accurately using CSS that looks like this:

```
#leftSide{
width: 200px;
}
#leftSide div{
border: 2px;
padding: 10px;
}
```

Using a fix like above, your div will always be 200 pixels wide (despite the border and padding) in *all* the browsers, regardless of quirks mode. Plus, your XHTML markup and CSS stays valid.

> **Container divs**: I find working with CSS and XHTML markup like this also keeps you from getting into other trouble; let's say we 'do the math' to figure our column widths and margins out, but then, either forget to account for borders and padding in the design or maybe just decide to add them later. In browsers like FireFox, a miscalculation or late addition like that will throw columns off, especially if their containing div is set to an exact width. This results in ugly, stacked columns. As you noted in Chapter 2, when we built the theme mockup, I like to use clean containing divs to *only* control placement, width, and margins. Then, I let inner divs (which will by default, expand to the width of the containing div) take on borders, padding, and other visual stylings. This is a good way to get your math right and keep it right, no matter what design additions may come later.

Your final alternative is to just create two stylesheets for your theme, one for general browser use and one for IE browsers, and let each browser call them in.

This isn't as bad as it seems. The bulk of your CSS can stay in your main CSS file, you'll then call in this specific IE stylesheet code below which will load additionally, only if the browser is IE.

In the IE stylesheet, you'll duplicate the rules and correct the properties that were not looking correct in FireFox. Because this stylesheet will load in *underneath* your main stylesheet, any duplicated rules will overwrite the original rules in your first stylesheet. The result is CSS styling that's perfect in FireFox and IE. However, if you run the CSS validator in IE it will alert you to the double rules.

In your `header.php`, `home.php`, or `index.php` template file (whichever file has your `<head>` tags in it), add the following code *after* your full stylesheet call:

```
<!--[if IE]>
    <link rel="stylesheet" type="text/css" href="ie-fix.css"
                            media="screen, projection" />
<![endif]-->
```

Is that a conditional comment?! Yes it is. In the past, your best-bet to loading in the proper stylesheet would have been using a server-side script to detect the browser with something like PHP. You could use a JavaScript as well, but if someone had JavaScript disabled in their browser, it wouldn't work. Not everyone can be a PHP whiz, hence, I advocate the just discussed method for loading in your two stylesheets with minimal hassle. This method is also best for keeping your two stylesheets as simple as possible (having a main one, then one with IE fixes), but you can apply *all sorts* of control to the conditional comment above, giving you quite a bit of power in how you dole out your CSS. For instance, you can specify what version of IE to check for (IE5, IE6, or IE7). You can also *inverse* the condition and only load in the CSS if the browser is *not* IE, by placing another exclamation point (!) in front of the IE, (for example, <!--[if !IE]>...<![endif]-->). Learn more about this conditional CSS tag at http://www.quirksmode.org/css/condcom.html.

You have to add that code in the theme's template file or files that contain the <head> tags. I usually put it in under my main stylesheet call. Yes, it would be nice if something like this could be implemented into the actual CSS file and then only parts of our CSS would need to be specific, and we'd only need to keep track of one file, but alas, you have to add it to your theme's header.php or files that contain the header tags.

Also, please note that while I advocate using the @import method for bringing in stylesheets, that method will not work within the <![if IE]> CSS check. Use the standard link import tags that are used in this include method above.

CSS troubleshooting technique: The best way to quickly get a handle on a rule that's gone awry is to set a border and general background color to it. You'll notice I did this in Chapter 3 to the initial layout. Make the color something obvious and not part of your color scheme. Often times, using this technique will reveal quite unexpected results, like showing that a div was inadvertently set somehow to just '500' wide instead of '500px' wide, or perhaps that another div is pushing against it in a way you didn't realize. It will quickly bring to your attention all the actual issues affecting your object's box model that need to be fixed to get your layout back in line.

The Road to Validation

You'll always want to validate your XHTML first. This is just as well because W3C's CSS validator won't even look at your CSS if your XHTML isn't valid.

Go to `http://validator.w3.org/` and if your file is on a server, you can just enter in the URL address to it. If you're working locally, from your browser, you'll need to choose **Save Page As** and save an HTML file of your theme's WordPress output and upload that full HTML file output to the validator using the upload field provided.

In our example above, you can see that we have a typo in one of our divs (looks like an odd **s** got in there somehow), and we have an image tag that doesn't have the proper closing (/) in it. Wherever possible, you'll note that the validator tries to tell us how to fix the error. Whenever a recommendation is made, go ahead and implement it.

We'll need to fix those two errors and run the validation again to make sure we're now validating. Don't just think you can fix the errors listed and move on without validating again. Occasionally, an error will be so grievous that it will block other errors from being picked up until it's fixed. Always **validate -> fix -> validate**, until you get that happy green bar telling you that you're good to move on.

Where's My Error? The validator tells us which line the offensive code appears in, which is why we love HTML editors that display the line number to the left in our **Code** view. However, once your theme is pulling in the content from WordPress, the line the offense appears in is not necessarily the same code line in your specific theme template anymore. So where's the error? Well, you have to know your template files enough to recognize where the error might be, for instance, I know that `<div id="footer">` is in my `footer.php` template file. Once I know the general file, I work around this by copying some *unique* text from the error, (in my case, `s>`). You can also use text from an `alt` or `id` tag within the reported object. Then, use the **Find** option in your editor to directly locate the error.

Ideally, when you run your XHTML through the validator, you'll get a screen with a green bar that says **This Page Is Valid XHTML 1.0 Transitional!**.

You can then move on to checking your CSS.

Open up another tab in your browser and go to `http://jigsaw.w3.org/css-validator/`. Again, same deal! If you're working off a server, then just enter the address of your CSS file on the development site and check the results. Otherwise, you'll have to use the **by File Upload** tab and upload a copy of your CSS file.

Here you'll want to see another screen with a green bar that says **Congratulations! No Error Found**.

If you don't get the green bar, the validator will display the offending error and again offer suggestions on how to fix it. The CSS validator will also show you the line of code the offense takes place on. This is handy as your stylesheet is not affected by WordPress' output, so, you can go right to the line mentioned and make the suggested fix.

Advanced Validation

Perhaps you've discovered (because you are talented indeed and would find something like this) that your XHTML and CSS validates, yet somehow something is still wrong with your layout. Or maybe, you're using some special JavaScripts to handle certain aspects or features of your theme. W3C's XHTML and CSS tools won't validate JavaScript. If you find yourself in this situation, you're going to have to dig a little deeper to get to the root of the problem and/or make sure all aspects (like JavaScripts) of your theme's files are valid.

Firefox's JavaScript/Error Console

You can use FireFox's JavaScript/Error Console (called the JavaScript Console in 1.x and Error Console in 2.x) to debug and validate any JavaScripts your theme is using. Go to **Tools | Error Console** in your browser to activate it; you can also activate it by typing **javascript:** into your address bar and hitting *Enter* on your keyboard.

You will be pleasantly surprised to find out that the console will also spit out several warnings and errors for CSS rules that the W3C's validators probably *didn't* tell you about. The Error Console does hold a *log* of all errors it encounters for all pages you've looked at. Therefore, the best way to proceed with the Error Console is to first hit **Clear** and then reload your page to be sure that you're only looking at current bugs and issues for that specific page.

Again, the Error Console will let you know what file and line the offending code is in, so you can go right to it and make the suggested fix. In my previous screenshot, it looks like the console is taking issue with the `thickbox.css` file (Thickbox is a web user interface feature we'll install and learn about in Chapter 9).

The Web Developer's Toolbar

This is a great extension which adds a toolbar to your Firefox browser. The extension is also available for the Seamonkey suite and the new Flock browser, both of which are like Firefox, powered by the open-source code of Mozilla.

Get it from `http://chrispederick.com/work/web-developer/`.

The toolbar lets you link directly to the DOM browsers and Error Consoles, W3C XHTML and CSS validation tools, toggle and view your CSS output in various ways, as well as just lets you view and manipulate a myriad of information your site page is outputting on-the-fly. The uses of this toolbar are endless. Every time I'm developing a design I find some feature, I'd never previously used, useful.

FireBug

A more robust tool is Joe Hewitt's FireBug extension for Firefox (there's a 'Firebug Lite' version for Internet Explorer, Safari, and Opera) (`http://www.getfirebug.com/`).

This extension is a powerhouse when combined with the features of the Web Developer Toolbar and even on its own will find them all—XHTML, CSS, JavaScript, and even little 'wierdo' tidbit things happening to your DOM (Document Object Model) on-the-fly. There's a variety of fun inspectors and just about all of them are invaluable.

 Linux and Firebug: "Firebug does work on Linux, but some distributions don't compile Mozilla correctly, and it is missing the components that Firebug depends on. Even more common is the case of individual Linux users compiling their own Firefox binaries incorrectly."--*Firebug FAQ* (`http://www.getfirebug.com/faq.html`)

Once you have Firebug installed into your browser, you can turn it off and on by hitting *F12* or going to **View | Firebug**.

My favorite Firebug features are the options for reviewing HTML, CSS, and the DOM. Firebug will show you your box models and let you see the measurements of each ledge. Plus, the latest version of Firebug lets you make edits on-the-fly to easily experiment with different fixes before committing them to your actual document. (There are features that let you do this using the Web Developer Toolbar as well, but I find the Firebug interface more in-depth—see the following screenshot.)

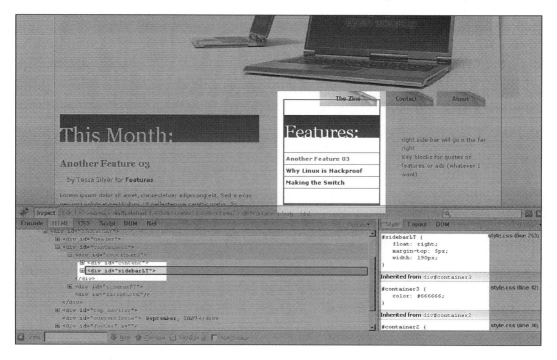

DOM? We've mentioned DOM a few times in this book. Learning about the Document Object Model can really enhance your understanding of your XHTML for WordPress themes (or any web page you design), as well as help you better understand how to effectively structure your CSS rules and write cleaner and accurate JavaScripts. Find out more from the W3Cschools (http://w3schools.com/htmldom/default.asp).

Extra Credit

If you want a better understanding of how all text browsers or some users on mobile devices are viewing your site (not including the new iPhone or iPod Touch and similar graphical interface mobile browsers), you can use Google's mobile viewing tool to give you an idea. This may help you visualize how to better arrange your site semantically for users in these categories.

To use this Google tool, type the following into your browser:

```
http://www.google.com/gwt/n?u=http://yoursitegoeshere.com
```

You'll now be able to see how your complete site looks without CSS styling. You can even turn off images. Use this to think about if your WordPress content is loading in logically and in the order of importance you prefer for your viewers. Also keep in mind that this is very similar to how a search engine bot will crawl your page from top to bottom and thus the order in which the content will be indexed.

What About the New Safari Mobile Browser?

The good news about your site and iPhone/iPod touch users is that the Mobile Safari (the mobile web browser Apple products use) is graphical. This means the browser seems to be able to take snapshots of your site fully rendered and shrink it down into the mobile browser allowing you to zoom in and out on the content.

Mobile Safari attempts to be standards compliant. If you've followed this book's guidance on creating W3C standards compliant XHTML markup and CSS in the creation of your theme, your WordPress site will most likely show up stunningly on an iPhone or iPod touch. The only major drawback I've seen in the Safari Mobile browser is the lack of Flash support, which is tough if your site has (or relies on) Flash content (such as embedded YouTube, Google Video, or Jumpcut.com clips).

Want more info on designing mobile devices? A List apart (as always) has some great info on designing for devices including the iPhone:
```
http://www.alistapart.com/articles/
putyourcontentinmypocket
```

Interested in Mobile Safari? Check out this great O'Reilly Digital ShortCut: **Optimizing Your Website for Mobile Safari: Ensuring Your Website Works on the iPhone and iPod touch (Digital Short Cut)** by **August Trometer**. It's a digital PDF you can purchase and download from inFormIt.com:
```
http://www.informit.com/store/product.
aspx?isbn=0321544013
```

Summary

In this chapter, we reviewed the basic process to debugging and validating your theme's XHTML markup, PHP code, and CSS. You learned how to use W3C's XHTML and CSS validation tools, and we further explored using FireFox as a valuable development tool by using its Error Console and available extensions like the Web Developer Toolbar and Firebug.

Next, it's time to package up your design and send it to your client!

5
Your Theme in Action

Now that we've got our theme designed, styled, and looking great, we just have one last thing to do. It's time to share your theme with your client, friends, and/or the rest of the WordPress community.

In this chapter, we'll discuss how to properly set up your theme's `style.css` so that it loads into WordPress installations correctly. We'll then discuss compressing your theme files into the zip file format and running some test installations of your theme package in WordPress's Administration Panel.

A Picture's Worth

Before we begin wrapping up our theme package, we'll need one more asset—the theme's preview thumbnail. Take a screenshot of your final layout, resize it and save it out to be about 200 pixels wide. Place your image in your theme's root directory structure and ensure that it's named `screenshot.png`.

WordPress offers previews of themes using the `screenshot.png`. It's in your best interest to take advantage of it. If you don't add a screenshot, WordPress will simply display a grey box. As mentioned, many shared hosting solutions pre-install many themes with their installations of WordPress. It can be difficult to scroll through all the textual names trying to find the theme you just installed by remembering its name. As most people will know what the theme they want to activate looks like, having the `screenshot.png` preview set up will help them out.

In a nutshell, there's not a whole lot involved in getting your new theme together and ready for the world. By using the default theme as our *base* for file reference and following good testing and validation standards, we already pretty much have a WordPress approved theme according to their **Designing Themes for Public Release** document.

For other tips, including how to promote your new WordPress theme, check out the document I just mentioned:

`http://codex.wordpress.org/Designing_Themes_for_ Public_Release`

Theme Packaging Basics

To make sure your template is ready to go public, run through the following steps before packaging it up:

1. Remove *all* the unnecessary files hanging out in your theme's root folder! As I work on a theme, I often rename the original default files to something like `orig_header.php`, and so on, for quick and easy reference of template tags which I know I'll want to use in my theme, but those must be cleared out before you package up. Be sure that *only* the files required to run the theme are left in your directory. Don't forget to **test your theme one more time** after deleting files to ensure you didn't accidentally delete a file your theme uses!

2. Open up the `style.css` sheet and make sure that all the information contained in it is accurate. I had you fill this out in the beginning of Chapter 3 when we were setting up our development theme directory, but I'll review it in detail below.

3. Create a `ReadMe.txt` file. Let your users know what version your theme is compatible with, how to install it, and if it has any special features or requirements.

4. Zip it up and put it out there! Get some feedback and install it in your client's installation of WordPress, upload it to your own website, or to your favorite user group, or post it directly on `http://themes.wordpress.net/`. The choice is yours!

Describing Your Theme

We very briefly discussed this in Chapter 3, just to get our development going, but let's review exactly what kind of information you can place into your stylesheet which will show up in the WordPress Theme Administration Panel. Essentially the first eighteen lines of the `style.css` sheet are commented out and without changing anything that comes before a colon (`:`), you can fill out the following information about your template:

1. **Theme Name**: This is where you'll put the full name of your theme.

2. **Theme URI**: Here you'll place the location from where the theme can be downloaded.

3. **Description**: It's a quick description of what the theme looks like, any specific purpose it's best suited for, and/or any other theme it's based on or inspired by.

4. **Version**: If this is your theme's first debut, you may want to put **1.0**. If the theme has been changed, had bug fixes, or reincarnated in any way, you may feel a higher version is appropriate. As this is essentially the same theme I've created for another project, I've just changed its color scheme, graphics, and reduced functionality. I've numbered it version **1.3** (for the three major visual revision processes it's gone through).

5. **Author**: Your name as the theme's author goes here.

6. **Author URI**: It's a URL to a page where people can find out more about you.

7. **The CSS, XHTML and design is released under __**: This is optional. You can use this area to describe any licensing conditions you want for your theme. The WordPress Administration Panel will not display it, though only people who've downloaded your theme and viewed the `style.css` file will see it.

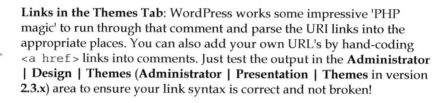

Links in the Themes Tab: WordPress works some impressive 'PHP magic' to run through that comment and parse the URI links into the appropriate places. You can also add your own URL's by hand-coding `<a href>` links into comments. Just test the output in the **Administrator | Design | Themes** (**Administrator | Presentation | Themes** in version **2.3.x**) area to ensure your link syntax is correct and not broken!

Licensing?

You'll find that most WordPress themes you found on the web either do not mention licensing or use the GNU/GPL license. If you're not familiar with the GNU/GPL license, you can learn more about it at `http://www.gnu.org/copyleft/gpl.html`.

You may wish to do the same with your theme, if you want it to be freely distributed, available to all, and changeable by all, with no permissions necessary as long as they acknowledge you.

If you've created a completely original design that you intend to sell commercially, or just want to be able to grant permission for any other possible use, you'll want to place specific copyright information and the name of the person or organization that holds the copyright. Something like © 2008 My Name, All Rights Reserved, is generally recognized as legal with or without any formal copyright filing procedures (but you should look up how to best formally copyright your design material!).

This book's theme has been leveraged from another project of mine for Packt Publishing for educational purposes. While the GNU/GPL license is more than adequate, its text is a bit more 'software-ish' and 'tech-heavy' than I'd like, so I'm going to redistribute the Open Source Magazine theme under a more general-public-friendly Creative Commons License (`http://creativecommons.org`).

I'll use the CC Labs DHTML License Chooser to assist me in selecting an appropriate license (`http://labs.creativecommons.org/dhtmllicense/`):

I'll of course allow sharing of the theme, and let others 'Remix', which means, derive new themes from this theme with proper credit. I will, however, prevent it from being *sold* commercially by another entity (commercial sites are welcome to download it and use it), and require the 'Share-Alike' option. This means that no one can legally take the theme package and offer it for sale or use it in such a way that it generates income for them without my permission. If they reuse or redesign the package in any other non-commercial way, they're free to do so; they're simply required to give me and Packt Publishing credit where credit is due.

My licensing agreement looks like the following:

"OpenSource Magazine WordPress Theme by Tessa Blakeley Silver is licensed under a Creative Commons Attribution-NonCommercial-ShareAlike 3.0 License."

The end result is a license that keeps to the spirit of the GNU/GPL license, but is much less vague. It tells the user upfront that it allows sharing, which is important to us for educational purposes and prevents commercial distribution without permission, and by requiring 'Share-Alike,' encourages a continued friendly WordPress-esque atmosphere of open-source collaboration. It also expressly states the version number of the license, making it very easy for anyone to look up and read in detail.

Create a ReadMe.txt File

You're now ready to create a `ReadMe.txt` file. ReadMe files have a long history with computers, often accompanying software installation. This has carried over to the web where anything that gets added or installed into a web service usually has a ReadMe file included. Many theme authors chose to make the ReadMe file a `.rtf` or `.html` file so that they can include formatting. You may deliver it in any format you wish. I prefer `.txt` files because it ensures that everyone can simply click to open the file, and the lack of formatting options ensures I keep my text as clear and concise as possible.

ReadMe files are not required for your theme to work, but if you want to have happy theme users they're highly recommended. Your ReadMe file is generally your first defense against theme users with installation and usage questions.

These are the basics of what you should cover in your WordPress theme ReadMe file:

- Inform theme users what your theme and template files will do (what kind of site it works best with, if any plug-ins work with it, if it's 'Widit-ized', and so on).

- Inform theme users of any deficiencies in your theme (any plug-ins it does not play well with or types of content it doesn't handle well, that is, I've seen good themes that don't do well with YouTube content due to column width, etc.).

- Discuss any specific modifications you've made to the theme (especially if it's a newer version of a theme you've previously released) and what files contain the modifications (it's always good to have comments in those files that explain the modification as well).

- Reiterate the basic steps for installing a WordPress theme (not everyone is keen on reading through WordPress's codex site and will know to unzip the theme or where to upload the file). Also, mention any special requirements your theme has. For instance, if you included some custom PHP code that requires special CHMOD (a.k.a. RewriteRules) or anything like that, specifically list the steps of action a user should take to get your theme running.

- As mentioned in Chapter 4, try and test your theme across platforms and browsers and mention any rendering issues that certain browsers may have on specific platforms.

- Reiterate the copyright information that you placed into your `style.css` sheet and provide your contact information (web page or email) so that people can reach you for support and questions.

> **ReadThisToo.txt:** As long as your ReadMe file includes the points just discussed, you're generally good to go! However, if you're gearing up to release themes for commercial sale, Tonya Engst's article on writing a ReadMe file is great. It's geared toward software developers, but can provide invaluable insight to your theme's ReadMe file (if the following URL is too long, you can also just go to `mactech.com` and use the Google search bar to search for *ReadMe file*).
>
> `http://www.mactech.com/articles/mactech/Vol.14/14.10/`
> `WritingAReadMeFile/index.html`

Zip It Up

We're now ready to zip up our theme files and test an installation of our theme package. Zipping is just the file compression type WordPress prefers, though it's suggested you offer at least two kinds of compression, such as `.zip` and `.rar` or `.tar`. If you're a Windows PC user, chances are, you're very familiar with zipping files. If you're a Mac user, it's just as easy. As a new Mac user, I was thrilled to discover its built-in support for creating zip archives similar to Windows XP (and I assume Vista). Select your theme's folder and right-click or *Ctrl-click* to select **Create Archive**.

Even if you're working off a server, rather than locally, it's probably best if you download your theme's directory and zip them up on your local machine. Plus, you'll want to test your install and almost everyone will be uploading your file off their local machine.

No Way to Zip?

If you're on an older computer and don't have compression software, you'll have to take a little tour of the Internet to find the very best zip solution for you. There are tons of free archiving and compression tools that offer the zip format.

So let's start with the obvious. If you don't have any zip compression tools, head over to `http://www.stuffit.com/`. You'll find that StuffIt software is available for Mac or PC and lets you compress and expand several different types of formats including `.zip`. The standard edition is most likely all you'll ever need, and while there's nothing wrong with purchasing good commercial software, you'll have plenty of time to play with the trial version. The trial for the standard software is 15 days, but you might find that it lasts longer than that (especially if you're patient while the **continue trial** button loads). If you're on a PC you also have WinZip as an option (`http://www.winzip.com/`) where again, you're given a trial period that does seem to last longer than the suggested 45 days.

WinZip and StuffIt are considered 'industry standard' software. They've been around for a good while and are stable products which, for under $50, you can't go too wrong.

> **Come on, where's the free open-source stuff?** If you must have truly free compression software and are on a PC, there is 7-zip (`http://www.7-zip.org/`). I've only minimally played around with **7-Zip**, but it does create and expand zip files and can even compress in a new format (called 7z) that gets better compression than standard zip files. Unfortunately, not too many people are readily using the 7z format yet, so make sure you're also creating a standard zip version of your theme when you use it.

Each compression utility has its own interface and procedures for creating a standard `.zip` file. I'll assume that you have one, or have chosen one from above and have made yourself familiar with how to use it.

One Last Test

You're now ready to test the package. Start from scratch. If at all possible, don't install the theme back into your sandbox installation (especially if it's on your local machine). If your sandbox is all you have for some reason, I recommend you rename your existing development theme directory or back it up (so you're sure to be testing your package).

Ideally, you'll want to install your theme on a web server installation, preferably the one where the theme is going to be used (if it's a custom design for a single client) or under the circumstances you feel your theme's users are most likely to use (e.g., If you're going to post your theme for download on WordPress's theme directory, then test your theme on an installation of WordPress on a shared hosting environment which most people use).

Don't assume the zip or compression file you made is going to unzip or unpack properly (files have been known to corrupt). Follow the procedure you know your client will be using or the procedure someone finding your theme on the web will perform.

- Unzip the folder (if applicable, download it from wherever it will be accessed from, and then try to unzip the folder).
- FTP the folder to the `wp_content/themes` directory.

- Go to **Administration | Design | Themes** (or **Administration | Presentation | Themes** in older versions of WordPress) and see if your theme is there.

- Select the theme and make sure it displays properly.

With the successful installation and testing of your theme, you now have an understanding of the entire WordPress theme development process—from conception to packaging.

Get Some FeedBack and Track It

You're not quite done! Great design doesn't happen in a vacuum. If you've developed your theme for private use by a client, then you've probably already gone through a rigorous process of feedback and changes during the theme's development. But if you're developing a theme for commercial sale, free distribution to people, or even just for yourself, you'll want to get some feedback. How much feedback is up to you. You might just want to email a handful of friends and ask them what they think. If you plan to widely distribute your theme freely or commercially, you really should offer a way for people to review a demo of your theme and post comments about it.

At first glance, if you're happy with something, you might not want anyone else's input. Having to hear criticism is hard. However, there's a scientific term called 'emergence', and it basically dictates that 'we' is smarter than 'me.' It's the basis behind a lot of things, from how ants form food routes for their colonies, to how people in urban areas create neighborhoods niches, and why the web is transforming itself into a huge social network. As far as feedback goes, if you have a group of people, guess how many jelly beans are in a jar, the average of everyone's answer will be closer to the exact amount than anyone's single guess. Now, design aesthetics are a lot more ambiguous than the correct number of jelly beans in a jar, but using this principle in receiving feedback is still something your theme can really take advantage of.

See how people use your theme. You'll be surprised the situations and circumstances they attempt to use it in that you would have never thought of on your own. After several feedback comments you'll probably be able to detect patterns: what kind of hosting they're using, what kind of sites (discussed in Chapter 2) they are applying it to, and most importantly, what about the theme is working for them and what drawbacks they are encountering.

You'll be able to offer version upgrades to your theme by being able to see if your theme needs any tweaks or additions made to it. More importantly, you'll also see if there's anything in your theme that can be parred down, removed, and simplified. Remember that *more* isn't *always* better!

Summary

In this chapter, we reviewed describing our theme in the `style.css` commented header and how to package up your finished theme into a working zip file that anyone should be able to upload into their own WordPress installation.

Congratulations! You now know about getting a WordPress theme design off that coffee shop napkin and into the real world! In the next few chapters, we'll get down into the 'real-world' nitty-gritty of getting things done quickly with our theme Markup Reference and Cook Book chapters. We'll cover the key design tips and cool 'HOW TOs,' like how to set up dynamic drop-down menus, best practices for integrating Flash, AJAX techniques, useful plug-ins, and more.

6
WordPress Reference

This chapter will cover information to help you with your WordPress theme development from the two CSS class styles that WordPress itself outputs to WordPress's template hierarchy — template tags and include tags — to a breakdown of The Loop along with a few other functions and features you can take advantage of.

I'll review the essentials with you and then give you the key links to the bookmark, should you be interested in more detail. Consider this chapter your 'cheat sheet'.

Class Styles Generated by WordPress

As we learned in Chapter 3, WordPress content is generated by those bits of PHP code known as template tags, that look like `have_posts()` or `the_category()` and so on.

There is one template tag that outputs *two* CSS classes — `wp_list_pages()` — which we first discussed in Chapter 2. In Chapter 3, we discovered if you pass this template tag a parameter of `title_li=`, WordPress assumes you're going to use the list as a set of navigation links, so it helps you out by adding the following class styles to the `<li>` tags generated by the template:

Class style	Description
page_item	Generated by the `wp_list_pages()` code. Use it to style and control the page menu items.
current_page_item	Generated by the `wp_list_pages()` code. Use it to style and control the currently selected main menu item.

WordPress even takes advantage of a CSS feature which lets you apply as many CSS class styles as you'd like to a *single* XHTML object. You simply leave a space in between each class name. The page list items are displayed as `<li class="page_item">` and the page that is currently selected displays as `<li class="page_item current_page_item">`.

By applying those two classes to the `wp_page_list()` template tag, WordPress enables you to create a very flexible navigation layout using pure CSS.

If you wanted to use WordPress as a full CMS, you could have *many* pages and their sub-pages displayed in a clean navigation menu. In fact, in the next chapter, I'll cover how to use this template tag's output to create a great dynamic drop-down menu.

Using the Template Selector Feature

In chapter 3, I intended my pages (**About** and **Contact**) to be static. So I removed the `comments_template` and `comments_number` template tag from the `page.php` template. But what if I want (or want my theme users to be able) to create a static page that lets users leave comments? This is easily achieved by creating a custom page template:

Time For Action:

1. Create a new file that contains the markup, CSS styles, and template tags you'd like your optional template page to have. I made a copy of my `page.php` and called it `page_dynmc.php`. I then copied the following comment loop back into it:

```
<div id="pagecomments">
  <?php comments_template(); ?>
</div>
<div class="comments"> <div class='commentIcon'><?php
comments_number('No Comments','<span class="bigNum">1</span>
response','<span class="bigNum">%</span> Comments'); ?></div>
<?comments_popup_link('Add Your Thoughts', 'Add Your Thoughts',
                               'Add Your Thoughts'); ?></div>
```

2. At the very *top* of the page, before any other coding, you'll want to include this comment inside PHP brackets:

```
<?php
/*
Template Name: Dynamic Page
*/
?>
```

3. You can then log in to your Administration Panel, and by going to **Administration | Write(or Manage) Page**, select the page you want to have a unique template, and underneath the editor window, select your new template from the **Page Template** selector drop-down:

Template Hierarchy

After the work we've done on our theme, you've probably noticed that certain WordPress template pages will override other template pages. Not being aware of what standard file names can override other file names within your template hierarchy can cause problems troubleshooting your template.

Essentially, you can have fourteen different default page templates in your WordPress theme, *not* including your `style.css` sheet or `includes` such as `header.php`, `sidebar.php`, and `searchform.php`. You can have *more* template pages than that if you take advantage of WordPress's capability for individual custom **page**, **category**, and **tag** templates.

For instance, if you've created a category whose ID is '4', and then created a template page in your theme called `category-4.php`, WordPress will automatically pull that template page in before accessing the `category.php` or `index.php` page when that category is selected. Same goes for tags; if I have a tag named 'office', and create a template called `tag-office.php`, WordPress will pull that template page in *before* pulling the `tag.php` or `index.php`.

 **Can't find your category ID?** If you want to create a specific category template page, but don't want to take time to use the the_ID() template tag to display the ID in your theme, and you don't have your WordPress **Administration | Settings | Permalinks** (or **Administration | Options | Permalinks** in 2.3.x) set to **default**, you can still *easily* figure out a category's ID number by using the Administration Panel's URI to discover the ID (this works for discovering the post and page IDs as well):

The following are the general template hierarchy's rules. The absolute simplest theme you can have *must* contain an index.php page. If no other specific template pages exist, then index.php is the default. You can then begin expanding your theme by adding the following pages:

- **archive.php trumps** index.php when a *category, tag, date*, or *author* page is viewed.

- **home.php trumps** index.php when the *home* page is viewed.

- single.php trumps index.php when an *individual post* is viewed.

- search.php trumps index.php when the results from a *search* are viewed.

- 404.php trumps index.php, when the URI address finds *no existing content*.

- page.php trumps index.php when looking at a *static* page.
    - ○ a custom template page, selected via the Administration Panel, trumps page.php which trumps index.php when *that particular* page is viewed.

- category.php trumps archive.php, which trumps index.php when a *category* is viewed
    - ○ a custom category-ID.php page trumps category.php, which trumps archive.php, which trumps index.php.

- `tag.php` trumps `archive.php`, which trumps `index.php` when a *tag* page is viewed.
  - a custom `tag-tagnam.php` page trumps `tag.php` which trumps `archive.php`, which trumps `index.php`.
- `author.php` trumps `archive.php` which trumps `index.php`, when an *author* page is viewed.
- `date.php` trumps `archive.php`, which trumps `index.php` when a *date* page is viewed.

You can find a detailed flow chart of the template hierarchy here:

`http://codex.wordpress.org/Template_Hierarchy`

WordPress's template tags go through revisions with each release. New and useful tags are introduced and some tags become deprecated (which means that one of the template tags has been superseded by a more efficient template tag). Tags that are deprecated usually still work in the current version of WordPress, but at some point their functionality will be removed.

Do not use a deprecated template tag in a new theme. If you have an older theme that now has depreciated tags, you'll want to update it to the new template tag equivalent and offer a new release of your template. Keeping up on the template tags page on WP's codex will help you keep your theme up-to-date.

Let's take a look at what I consider some of the more useful template tags to be. I won't list them all here, you can easily review them all in detail and clearly see what's been deprecated at `http://codex.wordpress.org/Template_Tags`.

New Template Tag in 2.5

I haven't found a need to use the new `wp_count_posts` tag in a theme yet, though, I can see how it would be primarily useful for plug-in developers.

Template Tag	Description	Parameters
`wp_count_posts()` **Sample:** `wp_count_posts('type', 'status');`	Returns the amount of rows in `wp_posts` that meet the `post_type` and `post_status` designated. **More Info:** `http://codex.wordpress.org/Template_Tags/wp_count_posts`	`post, page, draft, publish,` **Defaults:** post, `published`

Great Template Tags for Tags from 2.3

WordPress Version **2.3** saw the release of *five* new template tags. If you're interested in using the tags feature of WordPress then all five will be of interest to you.

Just a quick note: *tags* are not intended to replace categories. *Categories* provide a more hierarchical structure for your content. Tags are not hierarchical at all and function more like meta-information about your posts, letting you 'crosslink' them.

While you can assign multiple categories to your content (like placing a post in 'Features' and also in 'On The Web'), tagging additional keywords in that article, especially words that you might not want to set up a full category for, makes it easier for your site's users to find relevant information.

For instance, if I write two articles and one goes into 'On The Web' and another goes into 'Office Productivity', but both articles happen to talk about text-to-speech technology, I don't really want to create a whole category called 'text-to-speech' (especially as my site sparingly uses categories as 'monthly columns'), but I'll certainly add the tag to those items. This way, when someone who is interested in text-to-speech stumbles upon one of my articles, they can simply click on the tag 'text-to-speech' and be able to see all my relevant articles, regardless of what individual categories the content belongs to.

Adding Tag Display to Your Theme

In the interest of keeping things straightforward and concise, we didn't include tag-display capability to our theme in Chapter 3. That's OK, we'll do it now. This feature is *very easy* to add using the `the_tags()` template tag.

Within any pages that display The Loop in your theme, decide where you'd like your tags to be displayed. I prefer they be up top, under the author's name and category display.

I'll add the following template tag just *under* the author and category tags in my loop:

```
...<p class="authorName">by <?php the_author_firstname(); ?> <?php
the_author_lastname(); ?> for <?php the_category(', ') ?>
<br/><em><?php the_tags(); ?></em></p>
            <div class="entry">
```

The result is this:

The coolest new template tag is `wp_tag_cloud()`. It lets you easily generate one of those neat 'Web 2.0' text clouds that show all your tags and have the most used tags sized from larger to smaller accordingly.

The following are the 2.3 template tags:

Template Tag	Description	Parameters

the_tags()
 	
Sample:
`the_tags('before',`
`'separator', 'after');`
	Displays links to the tags a post belongs to. If an entry has no tags, the associated category is displayed instead.
	
	Note: Use this tag in The Loop. (see Chapter 3 for how to set up The Loop)
	
	More Info:
	`http://codex.`
	`wordpress.org/`
	`Template_Tags/the_tags`
		Any text characters you want to appear before and after the tags, as well as, to separate them:
		
		('Tags:', '|', '
		')
		
		Default: No parameters will display.
		
		Tags: `tagName, tagName`.

get_the_tags()
 	
Sample:
`<?php`
`$posttags =`
`get_the_tags();`
`if ($posttags) {`
`foreach($posttags`
`as $tag) {`
`echo $tag->name . '`
`';`
`}`
`}`
`?>;`
	This tag does not display anything by itself. You have to sort through it using a basic PHP statement— foreach—to display the information you want (see sample to the left).
	
	Note: Use this tag in The Loop. (see Chapter 3 for how to set up The Loop)
	
	More Info:
	`http://codex.`
	`wordpress.org/`
	`Template_Tags/get_the_`
	`tags`
		You can use the following parameters within the `foreach` statement to display the tag information:
		
		`$tag->term_id, $tag->name, $tag->slug, $tag->term_group, $tag->description, $tag->count`.

Template Tag	Description	Parameters

get_the_tag_list()
 	
Sample:
 	
echo
 	
get_the_tag_
list('<p>Tags: ',',
',', '</p>');
	This tag does not display anything by itself. If you use the PHP echo statement (see sample to the left), it can display XHTML markup of the tags assigned to the post.
	
	Note: Use this tag in The Loop. (See chapter 3 for how to set up The Loop.)
	
	More Info:
	
	http://codex.
	wordpress.org/
	Template_Tags/get_the_
	tag_list
		Similar to the_tags(), you can place any text characters you want to appear before and after the tags as well as separate them:
		
		    ('<p>Tags: ',',
		    ',', '</p>')

single_tag_title() **Sample**: single_tag_ title('This Tag: ');	Displays the title of the tag the user is viewing or sorting by. **More Info:** http://codex. wordpress.org/ Template_Tags/single_ tag_title	Any text characters you want to appear before the tag name can be added — ('This Tag:'). You can also add a Boolean of true or false afterward if you don't want the text to display — ('', 'false'). **Default**: The Boolean default is 'true' and no parameters will display — (no text) tagName.

General Template Tags—the Least You Need to Know

The following are the top WordPress template tags I find most useful for theme development:

Template Tag	Description	Parameters

`bloginfo()`
 	
Sample:
`bloginfo('name');`
	Displays your blog's information supplied by your *user profile* and *general options* in the Administration Panel.
	
	More Info:
	`http://codex.wordpress.org/Template_Tags/bloginfo`
		Any text characters you want to appear before and after the tags, as well as to separate them—`name`, `description`, `url`, `rdf_url`, `rss_url`, `rss2_url`, `atom_url`, `comments_rss2_url`, `pingback_url`, `admin_email`, `charset`, `version.'`
		
		Default: No parameters will display anything. You *must* use a parameter.

`wp_title()`
Sample:
 	
`wp_title('--',true,'');`
	Displays the title of a page or single post.
	
	Note: Use this tag anywhere outside The Loop.
	
	More Info:
	`http://codex.wordpress.org/Template_Tags/wp_title`
		Any text characters you want to use to separate the title—`('--')`.
		
		You can set up a Boolean to display the title—`('--', 'false')`.
		
		New in 2.5: You can decide if the separator goes before or after the title—`('--', 'true', 'right')`.
		
		Default: No parameters will display the page title with a separator if a separator is assigned its default to the left.

Template Tag	Description	Parameters

`the_title()`
 	
Sample:
`the_title('<h2>', '</h2>');`
	Displays the title of the *current* post.
	
	Note: Use this tag in The Loop. (See Chapter 3 for how to set up The Loop.)
	
	More Info:
	`http://codex.wordpress.org/Template_Tags/the_title`
		Any text characters you want to appear before and after the title— `('<h2>', '</h2>')`.
		
		You can also set a Boolean to turn the display to false— `('<h2>', '</h2>', 'false')`.
		
		Default: No parameters will display the title without a markup.

`the_content()`
 	
Sample:
`the_content('more_link_text', strip_teaser, 'more_file');`
	Displays the content and markup you've edited into the *current* post.
	
	Note: Use this tag in The Loop. (See Chapter 3 for how to set up The Loop.)
	
	More Info:
	`http://codex.wordpress.org/Template_Tags/the_content`
		As you can add text to display the 'more link', a Boolean to show or hide the 'teaser text', there is a third parameter for `more_file` that currently doesn't work— `("Continue reading" . the_title())`.
		
		You can also set a Boolean to turn the display to false— `('<h2>', '</h2>', 'false')`.
		
		Default: No parameters will display the content for the post with a generic 'read more' link.

`the_category()`
 	
Sample:
`the_category(', ');`
	Displays a link to the category or *categories* a post is assigned to.
	
	Note: Use this tag in The Loop. (See Chapter 3 for how to set up The Loop)
	
	More Info:
	`http://codex.wordpress.org/Template_Tags/the_category`
		You can include text separators in case there's more than one category— `('&gt;')`.
		
		Default: No parameters will display a comma separation if there is more than one category assigned.

Template Tag	Description	Parameters

`the_author()`
 	
Sample:
`the_author();`
	Displays the author of a post or a page.
	
	Note: Use this tag in The Loop. (See Chapter 3 for how to set up The Loop.)
	
	More Info:
	`http://codex.wordpress.org/Template_Tags/the_author`
		This tag accepts *no parameters*. Instead, use the full tags to get specific author information—`the_author_firstname()`, `the_author_lastname()`, `the_author_description()`, `the_author_nickname()`, etc.
		
		Default: This tag displays whatever the **Display name publicly as** setting in your user profile is set to.

`wp_list_pages()`
 	
Sample:
`wp_list_pages('title_li=');`
	Displays a list of WordPress pages as links.
	
	More Info:
	`http://codex.wordpress.org/Template_Tags/wp_list_pages`
		`title_li` is the most useful as it wraps the page name and link in list tags `<li>`. `.ext`, the other parameters can be set by separating with an '&': `depth`, `show_date`, `date_format`, `child_of`, `exclude`, `echo`, `authors`, `sort_column`.
		
		Default: No parameters will display each title link in an `<li>` list and include an `<ul>` tag around the list (not recommended if you want to add your own custom items to the page navigation).

Template Tag	Description	Parameters

`next_post_link()`
 	
Sample:
 	
`next_post_link('<strong>%title</strong>');`
	Displays a link to the *next* post which exists in chronological order from the current post.
	
	Note: Use this tag in The Loop. (See Chapter 3 for how to set up The Loop.)
	
	More Info:
	
	`http://codex.wordpress.org/Template_Tags/next_post_link`
		Any markup and text characters you want to appear — (`<strong>%title</strong>`).
		
		`%link` will display the permalink, `%title` the title of the next post.
		
		Default: No parameters will display the next post title as a link followed by angular quotes (>>).

`previous_post_link()`
 	
Sample:
 	
`previous_post_link('<strong>%title</strong>');`
	Displays a link to the *previous* post which exists in chronological order from the current post.
	
	Note: Use this tag in The Loop. (See Chapter 3 for how to set up The Loop.)
	
	More Info:
	
	`http://codex.wordpress.org/Template_Tags/previous_post_link`
		Any markup and text characters you want to appear — (`<strong>%title</strong>`).
		
		`%link` will display the permalink, `%title` the title of the next post.
		
		Default: No parameters will display the previous post title as a link preceded by angular quotes (<<).

Template Tag	Description	Parameters

`comments_number()`
 	
Sample:
`comments_number('no responses','one response','% responses');`
	Displays the total number of comments, Trackbacks, and Pingbacks for a post.
	
	Note: Use this tag in The Loop. (See chapter 3 for how to set up The Loop.)
	
	More Info:
	`http://codex.wordpress. org/Template_Tags/ comments_number`
		Lets you specify *how* to display if there are 0 comments, only 1 comment, or many comments— `('no responses','one response','% responses')`.
		
		You can also wrap items in additional markup— `('No Comments','<span class="bigNum">1</ span> response','<span class="bigNum">%</ span> Comments')`.
		
		Default: No parameters will display:
		
		No comments, or 1 comment, or *?* comments.

`comments_popup_link()`
 	
Sample:
`comments_popup_ link('Add Your Thoughts');`
	If the `comments_popup_ script` is *not used*, this displays a normal link to comments.
	
	Note: Use this tag in The Loop. (See chapter 3 for how to set up The Loop.)
	
	More Info:
	`http://codex.wordpress. org/Template_Tags/ comments_popup_link`
		Lets you specify how to display if there are 0 comments, only 1 comment, or many comments— ('No comments yet', '1 comment so far',
		
		'% comments so far (is that a lot?)', 'comments-link', 'Comments are off for this post').
		
		Default: No parameters will display the *same* default information as the `comments_number()` tag.

Template Tag	Description	Parameters

`edit_post_link()`
 Sample:
 `edit_post_link('edit', '<p>', '</p>');`
	If the user is logged in and has permission to edit the post, this displays a link to edit the current post.
	
	 Note: Use this tag in The Loop. (See Chapter 3 for how to set up The Loop.)
	
	 More Info:
	 `http://codex.wordpress.org/Template_Tags/edit_post_link`
		Any text you want to be in the name of the link, plus markup that you'd like to come before and after it—(`'edit me!'`, `'<strong>'`, `'</strong>'`).
		
		 Default: No parameters will display a link that says 'edit' with no additional markup.

`the_permalink()`
 Sample:
 `the_permalink();`
	Displays the URL for the permalink to the *current* post.
	
	 Note: Use this tag in The Loop. (See Chapter 3 for how to set up The Loop.)
	
	 More Info:
	 `http://codex.wordpress.org/Template_Tags/the_permalink`
		This tag has no parameters.

`the_ID()`
 Sample:
 `the_ID();`
	Displays the numeric ID of the *current* post.
	
	 Note: Use this tag in The Loop. (See Chapter 3 for how to set up The Loop.)
	
	 More Info:
	 `http://codex.wordpress.org/Template_Tags/the_ID`
		This tag has no parameters.

Template Tag	Description	Parameters

`wp_get_archives()`
 	
Sample:
`wp_get_archives('type= monthly');`
	Displays a date-based archives list.
	
	More Info:
	`http://codex.wordpress. org/Template_Tags/wp_ get_archives`
		You can set parameters by separating them with an '&' — (`'type=monthl y&limit=12'`).
		
		The other parameters are `type`, `limit`, `format`, `before`, `after`, `show_ post_count`.
		
		Default: No parameters will display a list of *all* your *monthly* archives in *HTML* format without before or after markup and `show_post_count` set to *false*.

`get_calendar()`
 	
Sample:
`get_calendar(false);`
	Displays the current month/ year calendar.
	
	More Info:
	`http://codex.wordpress. org/Template_Tags/get_ calendar`
		A Boolean value can be set which will display a single-letter initial (S = Sunday) if set to *true*. Otherwise, it will display the abbreviation based on your localization (Sun = Sunday) — (true)
		
		Default: No parameters will display the single-letter abbreviation.

Include Tags

The following is a list of all the tags and file names you can include into your theme:

Include Tag	Description
`get_header();`	Finds and includes the file `header.php` from your current theme's directory. If that file is not found, it will include `wp-content/themes/default/header.php` in its place.
`get_footer();`	Finds and includes the file `footer.php` from your current theme's directory. If that file is not found, it will include `wp-content/themes/default/footer.php` in its place.
`get_sidebar();`	Finds and includes the file `sidebar.php` from your current theme's directory. If that file is not found, it will include `wp-content/themes/default/sidebar.php` in its place.

Include Tag	Description
`comments_template();`	Finds and includes the file `comments.php` from your current theme's directory. If that file is not found, it will include `wp-content/themes/default/comments.php` in its place.

`TEMPLATEPATH`
 	
Sample:
`include(TEMPLATEPATH . '/filename.php');;`
	`TEMPLATEPATH` is a reference to the **absolute** path (not the URL path) to the current theme directory. It does not include a / at the end of the path. You can use it to include any file into your theme using the standard PHP include statement (see the sample to the left). This is how theme developers include the `searchform.php` file into their themes.

Custom Includes—Streamline Your Theme

In Chapter 3, we included our own custom sidebar using the WordPress TEMPLATE path inside a basic PHP include call. This technique can come in very handy in helping you streamline your theme's code and help keep it easily updateable.

For instance, my `index.php`, `page.php`, and `category.php` pages have different headers and slightly different uses of The Loop, but they all have the exact same page navigation code. This bit of code is small, yet if I ever want to tweak my internal navigation layout, I'll need to touch all three of those pages. Let's clean that up so that I only need to edit *one* page.

Time for Action:

1. Open up your `index.php` page and select everything from the `<div id="intTop_navlist">` down to the end div tag and `<!--//top_navlist-->` comment.

2. Cut that code out and paste it into a new template page—`navlist.php`.

3. Go back to the `index.php` and add this include file where all that code used to be:

   ```php
   <?php include(TEMPLATEPATH . '/navlist.php'); ?>
   ```

4. Test your internal page views out. You should see your layout working just fine.

You can now replace that same code in your `page.php` and `category.php` template pages with the `include` line you just created. Test out those internal page views again to be sure the `include` is working. Now any time you want to update your internal navigation, you only have to edit the `navlist.php` file.

You can get really granular with this technique. Feel free to really look through your theme and find ways to separate out parts into `includes` so that you don't have to worry about duplicating your markup.

The Loop Functions

Chapter 3 will really help you understand how to put each of these functions together into The Loop. The following is a description of each part of The Loop:

Loop Functions	Description
`<?php if(have_posts()) : ?>`	This function checks to make sure there are posts to display. If so, the code continues onto the next function below.
`<?php while(have_posts()) : the_post(); ?>`	This function shows the posts that are available and continues onto the next function below.
`<?php endwhile; ?>`	This function closes the `while(have_posts...` loop that was opened above once the available posts have been displayed.
`<?php endif; ?>`	This function ends the `if(have_posts...` statement that was opened above once the `while(have_posts...` loop has completed.

WordPress Core Functions

In Chapter 3, I wrote a custom display loop that showed the top five most recent post titles in my **Features** category. I used a WordPress function called `setup_postdata()`.

I mentioned you might notice that the `setup_postdata()` function isn't listed in WordPress.org's template tag reference page. Template tags are WordPress functions that are defined for use *specifically within themes*; the `setup_postdata` function is part of WordPress's core functions.

Core functions are primarily useful to plug-in developers and the developers customizing WordPress' overall functionality for themselves. Occasionally, as we discovered in Chapter 3, some of the functions can be useful to theme developers who want highly specialized functionality within their themes.

I won't take time to break down any core functions into a table, as most people won't really need these for their theme development. I just want to make you aware of the core functions, existence so that if you ever do find WordPress template tags to be limiting, you can see if getting creative with a core function might solve your problem.

The most useful core functions I've found as a theme developer are part of a class called `WP_query`. The `setup_postdata()` function is part of this class. Functions within this class let you call specific posts and manipulate post data and how it's displayed. You can find out more about this class at:

```
http://codex.wordpress.org/Function_Reference/WP_Query
```

 What's a class? This might seem to take us off topic from theme development, but it never hurts to understand WordPress a little better. You might only be familiar with the term 'class' as used in CSS. This is different. A *class* is also a term used in *Object Oriented Programming* (which is how WordPress is written using the PHP language). It can best be described as a 'package' or 'collection' of functions and rules that define what an object can have done to it and how that object will behave. *Objects* are instances of their class which hold actual data inside them (like post data, for example, in the case of WordPress). The data inside the object can be retrieved and manipulated via the functions available in that object's class (such as the `setup_postdata()` function).

Again, you can find out more about using the `setup_postdata()` function, as mentioned in Chapter 3, here:

```
http://codex.wordpress.org/Displaying_Posts_Using_a_Custom_
Select_Query
```

If you use PHP or are interested in it and would like to learn more about WordPress's core functions, you can find out more here:

```
http://codex.wordpress.org/Function_Reference
```

Summary

Aside from two style classes output by the page navigation template tag, WordPress lets you completely control your own XHTML markup and CSS styles. We've reviewed WordPress 2.0's template hierarchy, top template tags, as well as *include* and *loop* functions that will help you with your theme. I've also introduced you to the 'under-belly' of WordPress's core functions, should you choose to venture far out into the world of WordPress theme and plug-in development. Dog-ear this chapter and let's get ready to start cooking. First up: Dynamic menus and interactive elements.

7
Dynamic Menus and Interactive Elements

Most of the techniques I'm about to discuss in this chapter and the next one are often used inappropriately and needlessly, not-to-mention they can create issues with usability and accessibility standards, but if you haven't already been asked for one or more of these features, you will be!

Chances are half of every five clients has already asked you for drop-down menus, slick Flash headers, YouTube embeds, and other interactive content that they insist will give their site 'pizazz!'

My gut reaction (and probably yours) to anyone who utters the 'P' word is to pick up a heavy hammer! Unfortunately, the people who sling around such words, as Steve Krug notes in his excellent book 'Don't Make Me Think', are usually the CEO or VP,s and well, you know, people with money for the project. Wherever possible, you put down the hammer and give them exactly what they want—pizazz it is. Here we go.

Don't Make Me Think!: A Common Sense Approach to Website Usability is an excellent book on website design for usability and testing that anyone who has anything to do with website development or design can greatly benefit from. You'll learn why people really leave websites, how to make your site more usable and accessible, and even how to survive those executive design whims (without the use of a hammer). You can find out more at Steve's site (http://www.sensible.com/).

DYI or Plug-ins?

In this chapter and the next one, I'll discuss how to do some of these techniques yourself but will also direct you to comparable plug-ins, or in the case of more complex techniques, show you plug-ins that do the job and point you in the direction for learning more about doing it yourself. As to the question: Should I use Plug-ins or do it myself? That depends on a few things such as the following:

- Time available
- Your technical comfort level
- The level of control you want over the theme
- If your theme is unique for use on a single site or if you plan on a wide distribution of it

If you're new to web development, especially using PHP and/or you just don't have the time to create a completely custom solution, WordPress plug-ins are a great way for you to go. If you've been developing with various web technologies for a while and you want to have exact detailed control over your theme, then you should be able to implement and further customize any of the solutions discussed in these next few chapters.

The other consideration is the usage of your theme. If you're developing a theme that is for a specific client to be used only on their site, then you might want to implement a solution directly into your theme. This will enable you to have detailed control over its display via your theme pages and `style.css` sheet. If, on the other hand, you plan to sell your theme commercially or otherwise let it be widely distributed, your best bet is to make it 'Widgetized' and as plug-in friendly as possible. (By 'plug-in friendly', I simply mean, test it with popular plug-ins to make sure they work well with your theme.) This way, your theme users have greater flexibility in how they end up using your theme and aren't locked-in to using any features you've enabled the theme with.

Dynamic Menus?

This is the nice thing about WordPress—it's all 'dynamic', Once you install WordPress and design a great theme for it, anyone with the right level of administrative capability can log into the Administration Panel and add, edit, or delete content and menu items. But generally, when people ask for 'dynamic menus', what they really want are those appearing and disappearing drop-down menus which, I believe, they like because it quickly gives a site a very 'busy' feel.

I must add my own disclaimer; I don't like drop-downs. Before you get on to my case, I will say it's not that they're 'wrong' or 'bad', they just don't meet my own aesthetics and I personally find them *non-user friendly*. I'd prefer to see a menu system that, if requires sub sections, displays them somewhere consistently on the page, either by having a vertical navigation expand to display sub sections underneath, or if a horizontal menu is used, shows additional sub sections in a set location on the page.

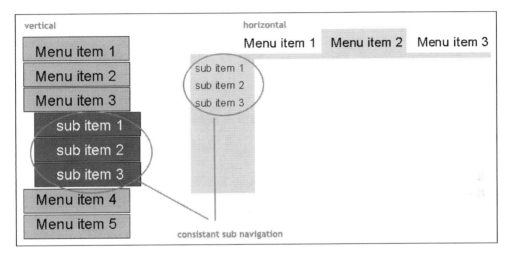

I like to be able to look around and see 'OK, I'm in the **New Items | Cool Dink** section and I can also check out **Red Dinks** and **Retro Dinks** within this section.' Having to constantly go back up to the menu and drop-down the options to remind myself of what's available and what my next move might be, is annoying. Still haven't convinced you not to use drop-downs? OK, read on.

Drop-Down Menus

So you're going to use drop-downs. Again it's not 'wrong', however, I would strongly caution you to help your client take a look at their target users before implementing them. If there's a good chance that most users are going to use the latest browsers that support current Javascript, CSS, and Flash standards, and everyone has great mobility and is 'mouse-ready', then, there's really no issue, go for it.

If it becomes apparent that *any* percentage of the site's target users will be using older browsers or have disabilities that prevent them from using a mouse and will limit them to tabbing through content, you must consider not using drop-down menus.

I was especially negative about drop-down menus as, until recently, they required bulky JavaScripting or the use of Flash which, does not make clean, semantic, and SEO-friendly (or accessible) XHTML. Until now. Enter the Suckerfish method developed by Patrick Griffiths and Dan Webb.

This method is wonderful because it takes valid, semantically accurate, unordered lists (WordPress' favorite!), and using almost pure CSS, creates drop-downs. The drop-downs are not tab accessible, but they will simply display as a single, clear unordered list to older browsers that don't support the required CSS.

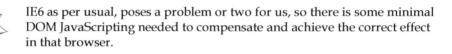

> IE6 as per usual, poses a problem or two for us, so there is some minimal DOM JavaScripting needed to compensate and achieve the correct effect in that browser.

If you haven't heard of or worked with the Suckerfish method, I'm going to recommend you to go online (right now!) and read Dan and Patrick's article in detail (`http://alistapart.com/articles/dropdowns`).

More recently, Patrick and Dan have revisited this method with 'Son-of-a-Suckerfish', which offers multiple levels and an even further parred down DOM JavaScript. Check it out at `http://www.htmldog.com/articles/suckerfish/dropdowns/`.

I also suggest you play around with the sample code provided in these articles so that you understand exactly how it works. Go on, read it. When you get back, I'll review how to apply this method to your WordPress theme.

DIY SuckerFish Menus in WordPress

All done? Great! As you can see, the essential part of this effect is getting your menu items to show up as unordered lists with sub unordered lists. Once you do that, the rest of the magic can be easily handled by finessing the CSS that Patrick and Dan suggest into your theme's CSS and placing the DOM script in your theme's header tag(s), in your `header.php` and/or `index.php` template files. Seriously, that's it!

The really good news is that WordPress already outputs your content's pages and their sub-pages using unordered lists. Right-click on the page links in Firefox to **View Selected Source** and check that the DOM inspector shows us that the menu is in fact being displayed using an unordered list.

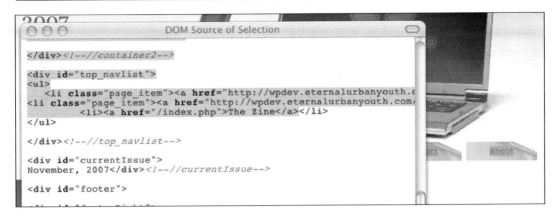

Now you can go into your WordPress Administration Panel and add as many pages and sub-pages as you'd like (**Administration | Write | (Write)Page**). You'll use the **Page Parent** tab underneath the editor (or on the right if your WordPress version is older than **2.5**) to assign your sub pages to their parent.

Once you've added sub pages to a page, you'll be able to use the DOM Source of Selection viewer to see that your menu is displayed with unordered lists and sub lists.

Applying CSS to WordPress

We're going to use the new and improved 'Son-of-a-Suckerfish' method so that our menu can handle multi-level drop-downs. To start, let's just take Dan and Patrick's suggested code and see what happens. Their unordered list CSS looks like the following:

```
#nav, #nav ul { /* all lists */
    padding: 0;
    margin: 0;
    list-style: none;
    line-height: 1;
}

#nav a {
    display: block;
    width: 10em;
}

#nav li { /* all list items */
    float: left;
    width: 10em; /* width needed or else Opera goes nuts */
}

#nav li ul { /* second-level lists */
    position: absolute;
    background: orange;
    width: 10em;
    left: -999em; /* using left instead of display to hide menus
    because display: none isn't read by screen readers */
}

#nav li ul ul { /* third-and-above-level lists */
    margin: -1em 0 0 10em;
}

#nav li:hover ul ul, #nav li:hover ul ul ul, #nav li.sfhover ul ul,
#nav li.sfhover ul ul ul {
    left: -999em;
}

#nav li:hover ul, #nav li li:hover ul, #nav li li li:hover ul, #nav
li.sfhover ul, #nav li li.sfhover ul, #nav li li li.sfhover ul { /*
lists nested under hovered list items */
    left: auto;
}
```

Now in WordPress, our menu item's `ul` is within a `div id` called `top_navlist`, And the ul id is reffered to as `navlist`. There may or may not be lots of other unordered lists used in our site, so we want to be sure that we *only* affect `ul`s and `li`s within that `top_navlist` id.

We'll simply tweak the CSS a bit to move items to the left (unfortunately, this works best with horizontal `Nav`s that are positioned from the left instead of the right) and make sure to add `#navlist` to each element in the Suckerfish CSS. Also, we already have a general `#top_navlist` and `#intTop_navlist` rule for the div, so we'll want to make sure that this only affects the `ul` within that `div` by making sure it's named `#navlist`. So our navigation CSS styles now look something like the following:

```
/*////////// NAV //////////*/

#top_navlist {
  position: absolute;
  top: 260px;
  width: 897px;
  text-align:left;
}

#intTop_navlist {
  position: absolute;
  top: 173px;
  width: 897px;
  text-align:left;
}

#top_navlist h2, #intTop_navlist h2{
  display: none;
}

#navlist{
  padding: 10px 10px;
  margin-left: 0;
  border-bottom: 1px solid #ccc;
  font-family: Georgia, Times, serif;
  font-weight: bold;
}

#navlist li{
  list-style: none;
  margin: 0;
```

```
      display: inline;
}

#navlist li a{
   padding: 11px 30px;
   margin-left: 3px;
   border: none;
   border-left: 1px solid #ccc;
   background: #8BA8BA url(images/oo_mag_main_nav.jpg) no-repeat top
                                                            right;
   text-decoration: none;
   color: #253A59;
}

#navlist li a:hover{
   background-color: #9E9C76;
   background-position: right -37px;
   border-color: #C5BBA0;
   color: #784B2C;
   text-decoration: underline;
}

#navlist li.current_page_item a{
   border-bottom: 1px solid white;
   background-color: #fff;
   background-position: right -74px;
}

#navlist li a:visited { color: #253A59; }

/*suckerfish menu starts here*/
#navlist li ul { /* second-level lists */
   position: absolute;
   border: none;
   margin-top: 10px;
   margin-left: 70px;
   left: -999em; /* using left instead of display to hide menus because
display: none isn't read by screen readers */
}

#navlist li ul li a {
   display: block;
   width: 150px;
   font-family: Georgia, Century Schoolbook, Times, serif;
```

```
    font-size: 12px;
    text-transform:none;
    font-variant: normal;
    font-weight:bold;
    border: 1px solid #666666;
    background-color: #ffffff;
    background-image: none;
}

#navlist li ul li a:hover {
    background-color: #cccccc;
    text-decoration: none;
}

#navlist li ul ul { /* third-and-above-level lists */
    margin: -1em 0 0 7em;
}

#navlist li:hover ul ul, #nav li:hover ul ul ul, #nav li.sfhover ul
ul, #nav li.sfhover ul ul ul {
    left: -999em;
}

#navlist li:hover ul, #nav li li:hover ul, #nav li li li:hover ul,
#nav li.sfhover ul, #nav li li.sfhover ul, #nav li li li.sfhover ul {
/* lists nested under hovered list items */
    left: auto;
}
```

Applying the DOM Script to WordPress

The last bit is the JavaScript so that the hover works in IE6. I call it DOM scripting or the DOM script, but it's basically just a JavaScript that rewrites your markup (how your DOM is being perceived by IE6) on-the-fly. This drop-down effect relies on the CSS hover attribute, IE6 only recognizes the hover attribute if it is applied to the a (link) entity. IE7 has fixed this limitation and works similarly for FireFox and other browsers. Dan and Patrick's script appends the additional .sfhover class to the li items in IE6 only.

You'll need to add this script to your index.php and/or header.php template pages, inside the header tags. The thing to remember here is that Dan and Patrick named their ul's id as nav and that's what this script is looking for. Our ul's id is named top_navlist, so by simply switching out document.getElementById("nav"); to document.getElementById("navlist");, you're good to roll in I.E.

The full script in your header tags should look like the following: (I prefer to tuck it into an `include` and place it in my `home.php` (or `index.php`) and `header.php` files with a JavaScript `inlcude`.)

```
<script type="text/javascript"><!--//--><![CDATA[//><!--
sfHover = function() {
    var sfEls = document.getElementById("navlist").getElementsByTagNam
e("LI");
    for (var i=0; i<sfEls.length; i++) {
        sfEls[i].onmouseover=function() {
            this.className+=" sfhover";
        }
        sfEls[i].onmouseout=function() {
            this.className=this.className.replace(new RegExp("
                                        sfhover\\b"), "");
        }
    }
}
if (window.attachEvent) window.attachEvent("onload", sfHover);
//--><!]]></script>
```

For demonstration purposes, I've kept the CSS pretty bare bones and ugly, but when we check this out in our browser we now see the following:

It's working! Remember with the preceding code, you can have drop-down menus that go three levels deep (Dan and Patrik's HTML Dog article shows you how to make it handle as many levels as you'd like).

Control those dropdown levels! As cool as SuckerFish drop-downs are, refrain from going overboard on those levels! Cascading levels can really become tedious for a user to mouse through and turn a site with a 'busy feel' into a total mess. You'll find that with a little care, you can easily organize your site's page content so that it only requires two levels. From there, if you *really need it*, you can add an occasional third level without creating too much user distraction.

Don't want all your pages to display? In our theme, we used the `wp_list_pages()` template tag to display our pages. You can amend the template tag with an `exclude` parameter, which will hide the pages we don't want to see, including their sub pages (example: `wp_list_pages('exclude=9&title_li=' );`). You do have to know what the page's id number is. (You can temporarily set your permalinks to 'default' to see the page's id number in the site's url). The pages themselves will still be available for viewing if you know their direct URL path. Read more about it at `http://codex.wordpress.org/Template_Tags/wp_list_pages#Exclude_Pages_from_List`.

At this point, all that's left is fixing up the CSS to make it look exactly the way you want. There you go, semantic, SEO, and accessible-as-possible dynamic menus in WordPress.

Drop-down Menu Plug-ins: Now you're probably already thinking: 'Wait, this is WordPress, maybe there's a plug-in' and you'd be right! By searching the 'Extend' section of the WordPress.org site, you'll find that there are a handful of WordPress plug-ins that allow for drop-down menus under different conditions. Ryan Hellyer has written a plug-in that uses the 'Son-of-a-SuckerFish' method that we reviewed in detail earlier. You can review it at `http://wordpress.org/extend/plugins/ryans-suckerfish-wordpress-dropdown-menu/`.

Ryan even offers a great drop-down style generator making it easy to get your menu's to match your theme's existing stylesheet (`http://ryanhellyer.net/dropdowns/`).

Flash-ize It

Adobe Flash—it's come quite a long way since my first experience with it as a Macromedia product (version 2 in 1997). Yet still, it does not adhere to W3C standards, requires a plug-in to view, and above all, is a pretty pricey proprietary product. So why is everyone so hot on using it? Love it or hate it, Flash is here to stay. It does have a few advantages which we'll take a quick look at.

The Flash player plug-in does boast the highest saturation rate around (way above other media player plug-ins) and it now readily accommodates audio and video, as video sites like YouTube take advantage of it. It's pretty easy to add and upgrade it for all major browsers. The price may seem prohibitive at first, but once you're in for the initial purchase, additional upgrades are reasonably priced. Plus, many third-party software companies offer very cheap authoring tools which allow you to create animations and author content using the Flash player format. (In most cases, no one needs to know you're using the $50 version of Swish and not the $800 Flash CS3 to create your content.)

Above all, it can do so much more than just playing video and audio (like most plug-ins). You can create seriously rich and interactive content, even entire applications with it, and the best part is, no matter what you create with it, it is going to look and work *exactly* the same on all browsers and platforms, period. These are just a few of the reasons why so many developers chose to build content and applications for the Flash player.

Oh, and did I mention you can easily make awesome, visually slick, audio-filled stuff with it? Yeah, that's why your client wants you to put it in their site.

Flash in Your Theme

A common requested use of Flash is usually in the form of a snazzy header within the theme of the site. The idea being that various relevant and/or random photographs or designs load into the header with some super cool animation (and possibly audio) every time a page loads or a section changes.

I'm going to assume if you're using anything that requires the Flash player, you're pretty comfy with generating content for it. So, we're not going to focus on any Flash timeline tricks or ActionScripting. We'll simply cover getting your Flash content into your WordPress theme.

For the most part, you can simply take the HTML object embed code that Flash (or other third-party tools) will generate for you and paste it into the header area of your WordPress `index.php` or `header.php` template file.

I use a very basic embed method based on the 'Satay' method (plus, this method works well with the Object Swap version check and ActiveX Restriction 'workaround' we'll get to in the next section of this chapter).

I like to wrap the object embed tags in a specific div id tag so that I can control its position via CSS.

Time For Action:

1. Using the `swf` file included in this book's code packet, create a new directory in your theme called `flash` and place the `swf` file in it. Then, include this code inside your `intHeader` div in your `header.php` template file:

```
<object data="<?php bloginfo('template_directory'); ?>/flash/
ooflash-sample.swf"
        type="application/x-shockwave-flash"
        width="338"
        height="150">
    <param name="movie" value="<?php bloginfo('template_directory');
                                ?>/flash/ooflash-sample.swf" />
    <param name="menu" value="false" />
    <param name="wmode" value="transparent" />
    <param name="quality" value="best" />
</object>
```

2. Add this id rule to your stylesheet (I placed it just below my other `header` and `intHeader` id rules):

```
#flashHold{
  float: right;
  margin-top: 12px;
  margin-right: 47px;
}
```

As long as you take care to make sure the div is positioned correctly, the object embed code has the correct height and width of your Flash file, and that you're not accidentally overwriting any parts of the theme that contain WordPress template tags or other valuable PHP code, you're good to go.

What's the Satay method? It's a slightly cleaner way to embed your Flash movies while still supporting web standards. Drew McLellan discusses its development in detail in his article:

`http://www.alistapart.com/articles/flashsatay`. This method was fine on its own until IE6 decided to include its ActiveX Security restriction. Nowadays, your best bet is to just implement the Object Swap method we'll discuss next.

Pass Flash a WordPress Variable

So now you've popped a nice Flash header into your theme. Here's a quick trick to make it all the more impressive. If you'd like to keep track of what page, post, or category your WordPress user has clicked on and display a relevant image or animation in the header, you can pass your Flash swf file a variable from WordPress using PHP.

I've made a small and simple Flash movie that will fit up right over the top-right of my internal page's header. I'd like my Flash header to display some extra text when the viewer selects a different 'column' (a.k.a. category). In this case, the animation will play and display **OpenSource Magazine: On The New Web** underneath the **open source** logo when the user selects the **On The New Web** category.

More fun with CSS

If you look at the final theme package available from this title's URL on Packt's site, I've included the original `ooflash-sample.fla`. You'll notice the `fla` has a standard white background. If you look at my `header.php` file, you'll note that I've set my `wmode` parameter to `transparent`. This way, my animation is working with my CSS background. Rather than beef up my swf's file size with another open source logo, I simply animate over it! Even if my animation 'hangs' or never loads, the user's perception and experience of the page is not hampered. You can also use this trick as a 'cheater's preloader'. In your stylesheet, assign the div which holds your Flash object embed tags, a background image of an animating preloading GIF or some other image that indicates the user should expect something to load. The user will see this background image until your Flash file starts to play and covers it up. My favorite site to get and create custom loading GIFs is `http://www.ajaxload.info/`.

In your Flash authoring program, set up a series of animations or images that will load or play based on a variable set in the root timeline called `catName`. You'll pass this variable to your `ActionScript`. In my `fla` example, if the `catName` variable does not equal `"On The New Web"`, then the main animation will play, but if the variable returns **On The New Web,'** then the visibility of the movie clip containing the words **OpenSource Magazine: On The New Web** will be set to 'true'.

Now, let's get our PHP variable into our swf file. In your object embed code where your swfs are called, be sure to add the following code:

```
<object data="http://wpdev25.eternalurbanyouth.com/wp-content/themes/
oo_magazine/flash/ooflash-sample.swf?catName=<?echo single_cat_
title('');?>"
        type="application/x-shockwave-flash"
        width="338"
        height="150">
    <param name="movie" value="http://wpdev25.eternalurbanyouth.com/
    wp-content/themes/oo_magazine/flash/ooflash-sample.
    swf?catName=<?echo single_cat_title('');?>" />
    <param name="menu" value="false" />
    <param name="wmode" value="transparent" />
    <param name="quality" value="best" />
</object>
```

Be sure to place the *full* path to your swf file in the `src` and `value` parameters for the embed tags. Store your Flash file inside your themes folder and link to it directly, that is, `src="http://mysite. com/wp-content/themes/mythemename/myswf.swf"`. I like to use the `bloginfo('template_directory');` template tag. This will ensure that your swf file loads properly.

Using this method, every time someone loads a page or clicks a link on your site that is within the **On The New Web** category, PHP will render the template tag as `myswfname.swf?catName=On The New Web`, or whatever the `$single_cat_ title('');` for that page is. So your Flash file's ActionScript is going to look for a variable in `the_root` or `_level0` called `catName`, and based on that value, do whatever you told it to do: call a function, go to a frame and animate, you name it.

For extra credit, you can play around with the other template tag variables such as `the_author_firstname()` or `the_date()`, for example, and load up special animations, images, or call functions based on them. Review the template tag options listed in Chapter 6 and experiment! There are a lot of possibilities for Flash control there!

Users Without Flash, Older Versions of Flash, and IE6 Users

What about users who don't have Flash installed or have an older version that won't support your content? By amending your object embed code with this following solution, your theme will gracefully handle users who do not have Flash (if you've used the overlay method above, they'll simply see the CSS background image and probably know nothing is wrong!) or an older version of Flash that doesn't support the content you wish to display. This method lets you add in a line of text or a static image as an alternative, so, people who don't have the plug-in/correct version installed are either served up alternative content and they're none-the-wiser, or served up content that nicely explains that they need the plug-in and directs them toward getting it. Most importantly, this method also nicely handles IE's ActiveX Restrictions.

What is the ActiveX Restriction? Last year the IE browser upped its security, so users now have to validate content that shows up in the Flash player (or any player, via MicroSoft's ActiveX controls). Your Flash content will start to play, but there will be a 'grey outline' around the player area which may or may not mess up your design. If your content is interactive, then people will need to *click to activate* it. This is annoying but there are workarounds for it.

Essentially, you need to include your Flash content via a JavaScript `include` file. I used to use my own custom JavaScript, which was great for new content, but not so great for all my old content that's already out there (who wants to go rewrite *all* their object embed tags as JavaScript `includes`?!). Recently, I've discovered the **ObjectSwap** method from **sitepoint**: `http://www.sitepoint.com/article/activex-activation-issue-ie`.

Time For Action:

1. It helps to understand a little bit of JavaScript, but even if you don't, this is a great script which will very easily allow you to activate Flash movies for ActiveX and make it much easier to update older content from past projects without striping out the original object embed tags. And because it's so simple, it fits right into a WordPress template page without any stress. You'll simply copy the JavaScript `include` line into your `header.php` and/or `index.php` header tags:

   ```
   <script type="text/javascript" src="<?php

        bloginfo('template_directory')?>/js/objectSwap.js"> </
   script>
   ```

2. You'll then include the `objectSwap.js` file with your theme template files.

3. Be sure to read the article at the link provided above. Download the example files from `http://www.sitepoint.com/examples/objectswap/objectswap.zip`.

More good news! It looks like Microsoft is planning to remove the *click to activate* requirement from IE sometime in 2008. You can keep up on this topic by visiting IE's blog (`http://blogs.msdn.com/ie/archive/2007/11/08/ie-automatic-component-activation-changes-to-ie-activex-update.aspx`). Even once this happens, as mentioned above, the `objectswap.js` is a great way to handle people who do not have Flash installed or a version that is too old.

Good Developer's Tip: Even if you loath IE (as lot of us as developer's tend to), it is an 'industry standard' browser and you have to work with it. I've found the Microsoft's IE blog (`http://blogs.msdn.com/ie/`) extremely useful in keeping tabs on IE so that I can better develop CSS based templates for it. While you're at it, go ahead and subscribe to the RSS feeds for Firefox (`http://developer.mozilla.org/devnews/`), Safari (`http://developer.apple.com/internet/safari/`), and your other favorite browsers. You'll be surprised at the insight you can glean, which can be in extremely handy if you ever need to debug CSS or JavaScripts for one of those browsers.

Flash in a WordPress Post or Page

For Flash content that's going to go into a specific WordPress post or page, you'll need to be sure to switch over to the **HTML (or Code in 2.3.x)** view and enter your object embed tag into the post or page where you'd like it to appear within your content. In the following screenshot, I've added the object embed tags for a YouTube video. (YouTube uses the Flash player for all their video content.)

> **New for 2.5!** The **Code** is now called the **HTML** view. WordPress **2.5** makes it even easier to add media—images, video, and audio. Just select the appropriate media type from the left side of the editor window.
>
> If you're using an older version of WordPress, just be careful. The first time you enter in custom HTML code into a post or page and hit save, the post will save and render your new code just fine. However, if you then edit that post, the custom code will look OK, as you edit it, but then for some reason, the custom code will be changed a little and might not display properly once you hit **Save**. (I believe it is because the WordPress editor attempts to 'fix' any code it doesn't recognize.) WordPress 2.5 seems to fix this issue and I have no problems editing and re-editing posts with custom HTML code tags. (The editor works a lot better with the Safari browser too.)

Again, if the user is browsing with IE6, then they will have to *click to activate*. The good news is the `swapobject.js` Javascript that we implemented above for your theme's headers can be leveraged *anywhere* on your site including these posts.

Yes, of course there's a plug-in: This won't help you too much if you're planning on Flash in your theme, but for Flash in your WordPress posts and pages, Jim Penaloza has written a great little plug-in using the **SWFObject** method detailed above. You can find out more about it here: `http://wordpress.org/extend/plugins/wp-swfobject/`

Want more Flash? Despite my warnings at the beginning of this chapter, if you still want to add more interesting Flash to your site, there's a host of Flash-based WordPress plug-ins that allow you to easily embed Flash content and features into your WordPress posts and pages. Check out the plug-ins directory at `http://wordpress.org/extend/plugins/search.php?q=Flash`.

Summary

In this chapter, we've looked at getting drop-down Suckerfish menus and Flash content quickly and painlessly into your WordPress theme and content. Next up—getting AJAX with dynamic interactive forms into your WordPress project.

8

AJAX / Dynamic Content and Interactive Forms

AJAX—it's the buzzword that hit the Web with a bullet in 2005, thanks to Jesse James Garrett, a user-experience expert who founded AdaptivePath.com. If you're totally new to AJAX, I'll just point out that; at its core, AJAX is nothing that scary or horrendous. AJAX isn't even a new technology or language!

Essentially, AJAX is an acronym for Asynchronous JavaScript and XML, and it is the technique of using JavaScript and XML to send and receive data between a web browser and a web server. The biggest advantage this technique has is that you can dynamically update a *piece* of content on your web page or web form with data from the server (preferably formatted in XML), without forcing the entire page to reload. The implementation of this technique has made it obvious to many web developers that they can start making advanced web applications (sometimes called RIAs—Rich Interface Applications) that work and *feel* more like software applications, instead of like web pages.

Keep in mind that the word AJAX is starting to have its own meaning (as you'll also note its occasional use here as well as all over the web as a proper noun, rather than an all-cap acronym). For example, a Microsoft web developer may use VBScript instead of JavaScript to serve up Access Database data that is transformed into JSON (not XML) using a .NET server-side script. Today, that guy's site would still be considered an AJAX site, rather than an AVAJ site (yep, AJAX just sounds cooler).

In fact, it's getting to the point where just about *anything* on a website (that isn't in Flash) that slides, moves, fades, or pops up without rendering a new browser window is considered an 'Ajaxy' site. In truth, a large portion of these sites don't truly qualify as using AJAX, they're just using straight-up JavaScripting. Generally, if you use cool JavaScripts in your WordPress site, it will probably be considered 'Ajaxy', despite not being asynchronous or using any XML.

We're going to take a look at the most popular methods to get you going with AJAX in WordPress using plug-ins and widgets to help you include dynamic self-updating content and create interactive forms in your WordPress site. While we're at it, we'll also look at some cool JavaScript toolkits, libraries, and scripts you can use to appear 'Ajaxy'.

 **Want more info on this AJAX business**? The w3schools site has an excellent introduction to AJAX, explaining it in straight-forward, simple terms. They even have a couple of great tutorials that are fun and easy to accomplish, even if you only have a little HTML, JavaScript, and server-side script (PHP or ASP) experience (no XML experience required) (`http://w3schools.com/ajax/`).

Preparing for Dynamic Content and Interactive Forms

Gone are the days of clicking, submitting, and waiting for the next page to load, or manually compiling your own content from all your various online identities to post into your site.

A web page using AJAX techniques (if applied properly) will give the user a smoother and leaner experience. Click on a drop-down option and the checkbox menus underneath are updated immediately with the relevant choices—no submitting, no waiting. Complicated forms that, in the past, took two or three screens to process can be reduced into one convenient screen by implementing the form with AJAX.

As wonderful as this all sounds, I must again offer a quick disclaimer. I understand that, as with drop-down menus and Flash, you may want or your clients are demanding that AJAX be in their sites. Just keep in mind, AJAX techniques are best used in situations where they truly benefit the user's experience of the page, for example, being able to add relevant content via a widget painlessly or cutting a lengthy web process from three pages down to one. In a nutshell, using an AJAX technique simply to say your site is an AJAX site is probably not a good idea.

You should be aware that, if not implemented properly, some uses of AJAX can compromise the security of your site. You may inadvertently end up disabling key web browser features (like back buttons or the history manager). Then there are all the basic usability and accessibility issues that JavaScript, in general, can bring to a site.

Some screen readers may not be able to read a 'new' screen area that's been generated by JavaScript. If you cater to users who rely on tabbing through content, navigation may be compromised once new content is updated. There are also interface design problems that AJAX brings to the table (and Flash developers can commiserate). Many times, in trying to limit screen real estate and simplify a process, developers actually end up creating a form or interface that is complex and confusing, especially when your user is expecting the web page to *act* like a *normal* web page!

You Still Want AJAX on Your Site?

OK! You're here and reading this chapter because you want AJAX in your WordPress site. I only ask you take the just discussed into consideration and do one or more of the following to prepare.

Help your client assess their site's target users first. If everyone is web 2.0 aware, using newer browsers, and are fully mouse-able, then you'll have no problems, AJAX away. But if any of your users are inexperienced with RIA (Rich Interface Application) sites or have accessibility requirements, take some extra care. Again, it's not that you can't or shouldn't use AJAX techniques, just be sure to make allowances for these users. You can easily adjust your site's user expectations upfront, by explaining how to expect the interface to act. Again, you can also offer alternative solutions and themes for people with disabilities or browsers that can't accommodate the AJAX techniques.

Remember to check in with *Don't Make Me Think*, that Steve Krug book I recommended in Chapter 7 for help with any interface usability questions you may run into. Also, if you're really interested in taking on some AJAX programming yourself, I highly recommend *AJAX and PHP* by Cristian Darie, Bogdan Brinzarea, Filip Chereches-Tosa, and Mihai Bucica. In it, you'll learn the ins and outs of AJAX development, including handling *security issues*. You'll also do some very cool stuff like make your own Google-style auto-suggest form and a drag-and-drop sortable list (and that's just two of the *many* fun things to learn in the book).

So, that said, you're now all equally warned and armed with the knowledgeable resources I can think to throw at you. Let's get to it; how exactly do you go about getting something 'Ajaxy' into your WordPress site?

Plug-ins and Widgets

In these next few sections we're going to cover plug-ins and widgets. Plug-ins and widgets *are not* a part of your theme. They are additional files with WordPress compatible PHP code that are installed separately into their own directories in your WordPress installation (again, not in your theme directory). Once installed, they are available to be used with *any* theme that is also installed in your WordPress installation.

Even though plug-ins and widgets are not the part of your theme, you might have to prepare your theme to be compatible with them.

Let's review a bit about plug-ins and widgets first.

Plug-ins

WordPress has been built to be a lean, no frills publishing platform. Its simplicity means that with a little coding and PHP know-how, you can easily expand WordPress's capabilities to tailor to your site's specific needs. Plug-ins were developed so that even *without* a little coding and PHP know-how, users could add extra features and functionality to their WordPress site painlessly, via the Administration Panel. These extra features can be just about anything—from enhancing the experience of your content and forms with AJAX, to adding self-updating 'listening/watching now' lists, Flickr feeds, Google Map info and Events Calendars; you name it, someone has probably written a WordPress plug-in for it.

Take a look at the WordPress Plug-in page to see what's available:

```
http://wordpress.org/extend/plugins/
```

Widgets

Widgets are basically just another plug-in! The widget plug-in was developed by **AUTOMATTIC** (`http://automattic.com/code/widgets/`), and it allows you to add many more kinds of self-updating content bits and other useful 'do-dads' to your WordPress site. Widgets are intended to be smaller and a little more contained than a full, stand-alone plug-in, and they usually display *within* the side bar of your theme (or wherever you want; don't panic if you're designing a theme without a sidebar).

If you're using WordPress version **2.2 and up**, the widget plug-in has become a part of WordPress itself, so you no longer need to install it before installing widgets. Just look through the widget library on WordPress's widget blog and see what you'd like! (`http://widgets.wordpress.com/`)

Trying to download Widgets but the links keep taking you to Plug-in download pages? You'll find that many WordPress Widgets 'piggyback' on WordPress Plug-ins, meaning you'll need the full plug-in installed in order for the widget to work or the widget is an additional feature of the plug-in. So don't be confused when searching for widgets and all of a sudden you're directed to a plug-in page.

WordPress Widgets are intended to perform much the same way Mac OS's Dashboard Widgets and Windows Vista Gadgets work. They're there to offer you a quick overview of content or data and maybe let you access a small piece of often used functionality from within a full application or website, without having to take the time to launch the application or navigate to the website directly. In a nutshell, widgets can be very powerful, while at the same time, just don't expect too much.

Getting Your Theme Ready for Plug-ins and Widgets

In this chapter, we'll take a look at what needs to be done to prepare your theme for plugins and widgets.

Plug-in Preparations

Most WordPress Plug-ins can be installed and will work just fine with your theme, with no extra effort on your part. You'll generally upload the plug-in into your `wp_content/plugins` directory and activate it in your Administration Panel. Here are a few quick tips for getting a plug-in displaying well in your theme:

1. When getting ready to work with a plug-in, read *all* the documentation provided with the plug-in before installing it and follow the developer's instructions for installing it (don't assume just because you've installed one plug-in, they all get installed the same way).

2. Occasionally, a developer may mention the plug-in was made to work best with a specific theme, and/or the plug-in may generate content with XHTML markup containing a specific CSS `id` or `class` rule. In order to have maximum control over the plug-in's display, you might want to make sure your theme's stylesheet accommodates any `id` or `class` rules the plug-in outputs.

3. If the developer mentions the plug-in works with say, the Kubrick theme, then, when you install the plug-in, view it using the Kubrick theme (or any other theme they say it works with), so you can see how the plug-in author *intended* the plug-in to display and work within the theme. You'll then be able to duplicate the appropriate appearance in your theme.

Installing the AJAX Comments Plug-ins

As I mentioned earlier, AJAX can really enhance the user's experience when it comes to forms. The most used form on a blog would be the comment form. Let's look at a plug-in that can really speed and tidy up the comment process. I'll be installing Mike Smullin's AJAX Comments Plug-in. You can get it from `http://wordpress.smullindesign.com/plugins/ajax-comments`.

If you can't spare the dollar that ol' Mike is asking for, you can also use Regua's **AJAX Comment Posting** plug-in (`http://wordpress.org/extend/plugins/ajax-comment-posting/`).

Regua's plug-in is good, but I just really like Mike Smullin's plug-in it's very light and works quickly. Well worth the dollar I spent on it. Here's the best part installing it:

Time For Action:

1. Unzip and upload the `ajax-comments` directory into the `wp-content/plugins` directory.

2. Go to **Administrator | Plug-ins** panel and **Activate** it.

3. Use it. That's it! The user sees their comment updated immediately with a note that the comment is awaiting approval. It's nice for the moment and they feel 'heard', but you might not ever actually approve the comment depending on its content.

Widget Preparations

Some plug-ins, like the widget plug-in (again you don't have to install this if you're using version WordPress 2.2 and up), do require your theme to go through some more formal preparation. You'll need to do the following to make your theme compatible with widgets (a.k.a 'Widgetized').

Time For Action:

1. Your side bar should ideally be set up using an unordered list format. If it is, you can add this code within your side bar: (If your sidebar is not set up using an unordered list format, ignore this step, but pay attention in step 3.)

```
<ul id="sidebar">
<?php if ( !function_exists('dynamic_sidebar')
        || !dynamic_sidebar() ) : ?>
 <li id="about">
  <h2>About</h2>
  <p>This is my blog.</p>
 </li>
</ul>
```

2. Because we deconstructed the default WordPress theme, based on the famous Kubrick theme, there is a `funcitons.php` file in our theme that already has the widgets registered for the sidebar. If by some chance you started completely from scratch or lost that file, you simply need to create a `functions.php` file in your `themes` folder and add this code to it:

```
<?php
if ( function_exists('register_sidebar') )
    register_sidebar(array(
        'before_widget' => '<li id="%1$s"
                class="widget %2$s">',
        'after_widget' => '</li>',
        'before_title' => '<h2 class="widgettitle">',
        'after_title' => '</h2>',
    ));
?>
```

3. My problem is that my sidebar format is much customized and it's not in a simple unordered list. Plus, I have two sidebars. I'd want the second sidebar that holds my GoogleAdSense to contain a widget or two, but not my 'Table of Contents' sidebar. Not a problem! The code we entered above in the `functions.php` file helps us with our more traditional div-header-list structure. Add this code to your non-unordered list sidebar:

```
<div id="sidebar">
<?php if ( !function_exists('dynamic_sidebar')
                || !dynamic_sidebar() ) : ?>
 <div class="title">About</div>
 <p>This is my blog.</p>
 <div class="title">Links</div>
 <ul>
  <li><a href="http://example.com">Example</a></li>
 </ul>
<?php endif; ?>
</div>
```

4. You've got two sidebars and you want them both to be dynamic? Instead of `register_sidebar()`, use `register_sidebars(n)`, where n is the number of sidebars. Place them before the array bit of code if you're using a non-unordered list sidebar, like so:

```
<?php
if ( function_exists('register_sidebar') )
    register_sidebar(n, array(
        'before_widget' => '<li id="%1$s"
                  class="widget %2$s">',
        'after_widget' => '</li>',
        'before_title' => '<h2 class="widgettitle">',
        'after_title' => '</h2>',
    ));
?>
```

Then place the appropriate number in the `dynamic_sidebar()` function, starting with 1. For example:

```
<div id="sidebar1">
<?php if ( !function_exists('dynamic_sidebar')
                || !dynamic_sidebar(1) ) : ?>
<div class="title">About</div>
```

Your theme is now 'Widgetized'. For those of you who are looking forward to creating commercial themes be sure to tell everyone your theme is widget-friendly.

Like Widgets? Learn all about how to control their display in your theme and even develop your own. Check out AUTOMATTIC's Widget API Documentation at `http://automattic.com/code/widgets/api/`.

Additional Considerations: There are no concrete standards for widgets as of yet (though, the W3C is working on it (`http://www.w3.org/TR/widgets/`). Many WordPress widgets, like Google Reader, are flexible and can handle just about any size column. Some widgets may require a minimum column size! You may need to adjust your theme if the widget has an inflexible size. Some widgets (especially the ones that display monetized ads for your site) have display requirements and restrictions. Be sure to thoroughly investigate and research any widget you're interested in installing on your site.

Installing the Google Reader Widget

I do a lot of online reading, thank goodness for RSS feeds. I used to load-in all sorts of RSS feeds to my site to show people what I was reading, but that's not very accurate. It only shows what sites I usually go to, and what I *might* have read on that site. With all the new sites and blogs coming and going, I'd have old feeds left on my site, it got to be ugly, and I eventually stripped them all out.

Google Reader has a *shared* feed that lets people know exactly what I really have been reading and interested in. Thanks to this handy widget by James Wilson, I can share what I'm really reading, in real-time, quickly and easily. Once your theme is widget-compatible, it's pretty much just as simple to get a widget up and running as a plug-in. Get the Google Reader Widget from `http://wordpress.org/extend/plugins/google-reader-widget/`.

Time For Action:

1. Unzip and drop `googlereader.php` file into the `wp-content/plugins` directory. (Depending on the widget, be sure to read the author's instructions. Some will want you to install to the `wp-content/plugins` directory and some will want you to install to the `wp-content/plugins/widgets` directory. You might have to create the widget directory.)

2. Go to **Administration | Plug-ins** and **Activate** it.

3. Go to **Administration | Presentation | Widgets** and drag the widget to your *sidebar* area.

4. View it on your site.

I ran into a snag with the Google Reader Widget:

I had to read the FAQ for the Google Reader Widget to learn that my hosting provider doesn't approve of the `file_get_contents()` method (http://wordpress.org/extend/plugins/google-reader-widget/faq/). So I had to modify my `googlereader.php` file at line 57 with the following workaround the widget author recommended:

```
$ch = curl_init();
$timeout = 5; // set to zero for no timeout
curl_setopt ($ch, CURLOPT_URL, $uri);
curl_setopt ($ch, CURLOPT_RETURNTRANSFER, 1);
curl_setopt ($ch, CURLOPT_CONNECTTIMEOUT, $timeout);
$stories = curl_exec($ch);
curl_close($ch);
```

After making this tweak, the Widget worked fine:

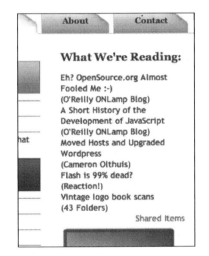

AJAX–It's Not Just for Your Site Users

I've already mentioned how, when applied properly, AJAX can aid in interface usability. WordPress attempts to take advantage of this within its Administration Panel by enhancing it with relevant information and compressing multiple page forms into one single-screen area. The following is a quick look at how WordPress uses AJAX to enhance it's Administration Panel forms:

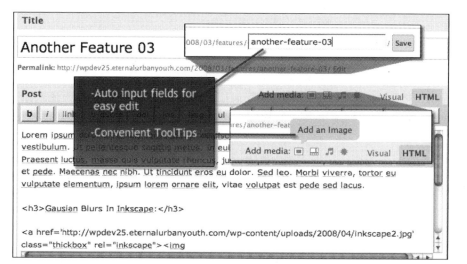

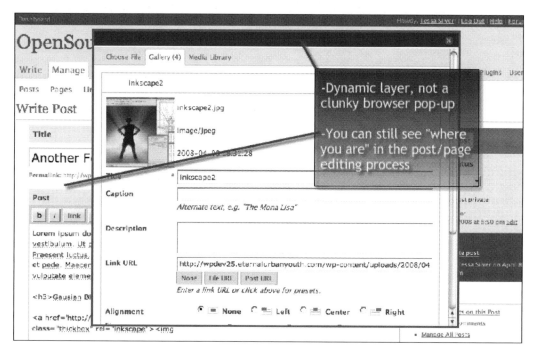

Even if you haven't upgraded to WordPress **2.5**, WordPress **2.3** makes use of AJAX on the widgets panel, allowing you to easily drag-and-drop to add and arrange your sidebar widgets. (For some reason, this has been redesigned in **2.5**; I would have preferred if it had stayed the same).

pageMash

In addition to finding plug-ins and widgets that enhance your theme, you should consider looking for plug-ins that enhance your administration experience of WordPress! For example, if your WordPress site has a lot of pages and/or you display your page links as drop-down menus, as discussed in Chapter 7, then, Joel Starnes pageMash plug-in is for you.

pageMash is a great little plug-in that uses the MooTools framework and Moo. fx library. Instead of having to go into each *individual* page's editor view and then use the **Page Parent** view to manipulate your pages around into your hierarchical structure, this plug-in lets you reorder and assign pages as parents and sub-pages on-the-fly.

Time For Action:

1. Download the pageMash plug-in from: `http://wordpress.org/extend/plugins/pagemash/`.

2. Unzip the files and upload the `pagemash` directory to your `/wp-content/plugins/` directory.

3. Go to **Administration | Plug-ins** and **Activate** it. pageMash will then show up under the **Administration | Manage tag**.

I hope you can get an idea by the following screenshot about how much easier and quicker it is to arrange your WordPress pages with pageMash.

The AJAX Factor

Aside from the many-interface enhancing, time-saving benefits of Ajax, sometimes you do just want to 'wow' your site visitors. It's easy to give your site an 'Ajaxy' feel, regardless of asynchronously updating it with server-side XML, just by sprucing up your interface with some snappy JavaScripts. The easiest way to get many of these effects is to reference a JavaScript library (sometimes called a toolkit or framework, depending on how robust the provider feels the code is). A few of the leading favorites in the AJAX community (in no particular order) are:

1. Script.aculo.us: (`http://script.aculo.us/`)
2. Prototype: (`http://www.prototypejs.org/`)
3. jQuery: (`http://jquery.com/`)

There's also:

4. MooTools: (`http://mootools.net/`)
5. Moo.fx: (`http://moofx.mad4milk.net/`)

Prototype is more of a framework and Script.aculo.us is more of an add-on toolkit or set of libraries for neat effects. In fact, Script.aculo.us references the Prototype framework, so your best bet is probably to use Script.aculo.us, but if you do work with it, *be sure* to check out Prototype's site and try to understand what that framework does.

Moo.fx is the smallest JavaScript effects library (boasting a 3k footprint), but again, it needs to be supported by the MooTools or Prototype frameworks.

jQuery is my personal favorite. It pretty much stands on its own without needing to be backed up by a more robust framework (like Prototype), but you can still do some very robust things with it, manipulating data and the DOM, plus it's packed with neat and cute visual effects, similar to Script.aculo.us.

Using JavaScript libraries like the above, you'll be able to implement their features and effects with simple calls into your WordPress posts and pages.

JavaScript Component Scripts

The fun doesn't stop there! What's that? You don't have time to go read up on how to use a JavaScript library like jQuery? Never fear! There are many other JavaScript effect components and libraries that are built using the libraries above. One of the most popular scripts out there that makes a big hit on any website is **Lightbox JS**:

```
http://www.huddletogether.com/projects/lightbox2/
```

Lightbox JS is a 'simple, unobtrusive script used to overlay images on the current page.' It's great, but it uses both the Prototype and Script.aculo.us libraries to achieve its effects. I also found that Lightbox was limited to only displaying images and a hair difficult to manipulate it to handle anything more than that. What if I wanted to display XHTML text, or markup containing YouTube videos, maybe even make an AJAX request to the server?

Enter **Thickbox**: `http://jquery.com/demo/thickbox/`

Thickbox is very similar to Lightbox JS. It uses only the jQuery library, and in addition to handling images similar to Lightbox JS, it can also handle in-line content, iFrame content, and AJAX content (be sure to check out the examples on the ThickBox page!). The downside—Thickbox doesn't do that *smooth* animation that Lightbox JS (version 2) does when images are different sizes. This is the trade-off I made when I decided it was more important to be able to display more than just images in my OpenSource Magazine theme.

Depending on your theme's design and what type of blog or site you're creating it for, you may opt to use Lightbox instead or something all together different! It's your theme, don't feel limited to what I specifically discuss in this book. I'll walk you through the process of installing ThickBox, but many 'Ajaxy' scripts that use these JavaScript libraries/frameworks are installed similarly. Just follow the instructions in the ReadMe files and you're on your way to an enhanced theme.

Time For Action:

1. This is an extremely easy-to-implement script. After downloading it, add the key js and CSS files to your WordPress theme's home.php and header.php files using the bloginfo template tag to target your theme:

```
<script type="text/javascript" src="<?php bloginfo
('template_directory'); ?>/js/jquery.js"></script>
<script type="text/javascript" src="<?php bloginfo
('template_directory'); ?>/js/thickbox.js"></script>
```

2. You'll also add in a call to the ThickBox CSS file:

```
<style type="text/css" media="all">@import "<?php bloginfo
('template_directory'); ?>/thickbox.css";</style>
```

3. Don't forget to upload the loadingAnimation.gif and macFFBgHack.png images to your theme directory and update the thickbox.js and thickbox.css files as per the ReadMe file instructions.

4. Then, you can create a post (or page) in your Administration Panel and using the Code View add in basic href links around your image tags, like so:

```
<a href='/wp-content/uploads/2008/04/inkscape2.jpg'
class="thickbox" rel="inkscape"><img src="/wp-content/
uploads/2008/04/inkscape2-150x150.jpg" alt="" title="inkscape2"
width="150" height="150" class="alignnone size-thumbnail
wp-image-15" /></a>
<a href='/wp-content/uploads/2008/04/inkscape1.jpg'
class="thickbox" rel="inkscape"><img src="/wp-content/
uploads/2008/04/inkscape1-150x150.jpg" alt="" title="inkscape1"
width="150" height="150" class="alignnone size-thumbnail
wp-image-14" /></a>
```

I uploaded the images via WordPress's built-in up-loader and let WordPress create the thumbnails; I just added the captions to the title attribute, the rel attribute and the thickbox class by hand.

That's it!

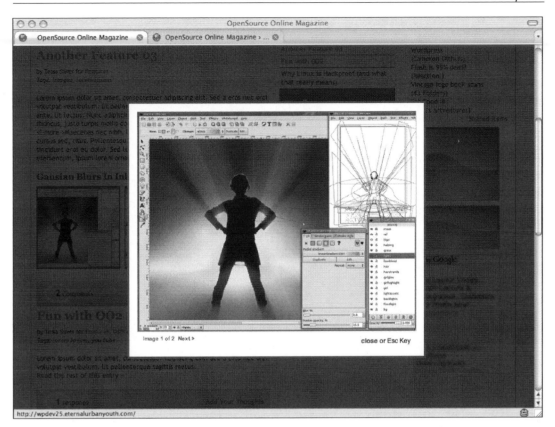

Summary

In this chapter, we reviewed a few ways to take advantage of AJAX on your WordPress site. We 'Wigitized' our theme and downloaded and installed a couple of useful plug-ins, and looked at using jQuery and ThickBox to enhance post and page content. Up next—let's take a look at some final design tips to working with WordPress.

9

Design Tips for Working with WordPress

Alright, for this last chapter, let's sum things up by giving you a few final design tips, tricks, and troubleshooting ideas to take with you into your future WordPress theme designs. As we've gone through this book there are quite a few tips that have been given to you along the way. Here are the top four to remember:

1. **Create and keep lists**: Check lists, color lists, font lists, image treatment lists. Keep all of these handy from your initial design phase. You'll find them to be useful and excellent inspiration for your designs to come.

2. **Design for FireFox first, then, fix for IE**: Firefox is more than a browser preference; it's a true web designer and developer's tool.

3. **Validate your XHTML and CSS... often**: The more stable your markup and CSS, the less hacks and fixes you'll need to make.

4. **Consider usability issues when implementing site enhancements**: Steve Krug is a cool guy. Moreover, good usability naturally lends itself to great design.

With that said, let's just go over a few last design techniques that any good designer wants in their arsenal these days.

The Cool Factor

Next, I'll go through what I feel are the most popular tricks used in website design today. After that, we'll take a look at some interesting samples of unique design ideas and how theme authors approached achieving them. Most techniques are easily incorporated into WordPress as they're handled one hundred percent via CSS. A few items will require you to think and plan ahead, as you'll need to make sure the WordPress theme code accommodates the effect. The best thing is, if you can implement these techniques into a WordPress theme, you can implement them into any website.

First off, we've already looked at several 'cool factor' techniques that are very popular in web design today. Among these techniques are using floats to create a three column layout complete with header and footer, along with a two column internal page layout. We've looked at styling lists with CSS (essential, as WordPress outputs a *lot* of lists). And we've also covered using the CSS hover property for our drop-down menus, which could be applied to text or used with images for a rollover effect without the use of (or with minimal use of) JavaScript.

Get good with backgrounds! If you haven't already realized this by now, about ninety eight percent of the CSS that will make your WordPress theme look great is dependent on how creative you get with images and the background properties of your XHTML objects, classes, and id rules. From page header backgrounds to data table spruce ups, rounded corners and fancy text (as you'll find out about in a minute), knowing how to really control and manipulate background colors and images via CSS is key. Check out `http://w3schools.com/CSS/CSS_background.asp` to learn the ins and outs of this CSS property.

Rounded Corners

Rounded corners have been pretty popular the past few years, to the point that many sites have been accused of incorporating them just beacuase they seemed 'Web 2.0-ish'. Fads aside, rounded corners are occasionally just flat going to work well with a design (they're great for implying happy-friendly-ish tones and/or retro styles), so you might as well know how to incorporate them into your WordPress theme.

The Classic – All Four Corners

Ideally, you'll wrap your WordPress template tag in enough div tags to be able to create a round cornered object that is flexible enough to scale horizontally and vertically. You can also use heading tags or probably any other XHTML tag that occurs in the element.

Really understanding rounded corners in a table-less design: If you haven't noticed by now, I'm a fan of aListApart.com, so I'll leave it to these trusted experts to give you the complete low-down on the details outs of making rounded corner boxes with pure CSS:

```
http://www.alistapart.com/articles/customcorners/
```

Also, there are many rounded corner generator sites out there which will do a lot of the work for you. If you're getting comfortable with CSS and XHTML markup, you'll be able to take the generated code from one of these sites and 'massage' the CSS into your WordPress `style.css`. Roundedcornr.com is my favorite:

```
http://www.roundedcornr.com/
```

To start, just make four rounded corner images named `left-bot.gif`, `right-bot.gif`, `left-top.gif`, and `right-top.gif` respectively (or generate them at roundedcornr.com). And using a class name called `.sidebarItem` (you can name this class whatever you'd like), reference the images via background parameters in your CSS like so:

```
.sidebarItem {
   background: #cccccc;
   background: url(../images/left-top.gif) no-repeat top left;
   /*be sure to set your
   preferred font requirements*/
}
.sidebarItem div {
   background: url(../images/right-top.gif) no-repeat top right;
}
.sidebarItem div div {
   background: url(../images/left-bot.gif) no-repeat bottom left;
}
.sidebarItem div div div {
   background: url(roundedcornr_170953_br.png) no-repeat bottom
                                                          right;
}
.sidebarItem div div div, .sidebarItem div div, .sidebarItem div,
.module{
   width: 100%;
   height: 30px;
   font-size: 1px;
}
.sidebarItem {
  margin: 0 30px;
}
```

The following is an example of the markup you should wrap your template tag(s) in:

```
<div class="sidebarItem"> <!--//left-top.gif-->f
<div> <!--//right-top.gif-->
    <div> <!--//left-bot.gif-->
        <div> <!--//right-bot.gif-->
            <h3>Header</h3>
                Content the Template Tag outputs goes in here
        </div>
    </div>
</div>
</div>
```

Your end result should be something that looks like the following:

The Two Image Cheat

I'll be honest; I'm on the cheater's band wagon when it comes to rounded corners. I often create locked-width designs so I always know exactly how much room my columns can take up, and they only need to be able to expand vertically.

More aListApart: Again aListApart.com comes in with a great take on this two image process, along with some great tips for creating the corners in your favorite graphic program:

`http://www.alistapart.com/articles/mountaintop/`

This rounded corner fix *only works* for a *set width* with a variable height. That means, how wide you make your graphic, is as wide as your *outer div* should be. So, if you know the width of your columns and just need the height to expand, you can do this two image cheat by only making a top image and an extended bottom image like so:

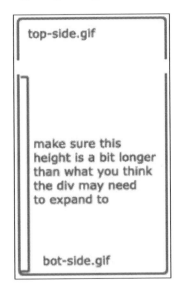

Test this technique! In the previous graphic, I mention to **make sure this height is a bit longer than what you think the div may need to expand to**. Once you have it implemented, try it out in different browsers and set your browser's default type to different sizes. If someone has their browser set to very large type, this effect can be easily broken!

Next reference the images in your CSS (note how much simpler the CSS becomes):

```
.sidebarItem {
   margin:0 0 10px 0;
   padding:0 0 10px 0;
   width: 150px;
   background:url(../images/bot-side.gif) bottom left no-repeat;
     /*be sure to set your
```

```
        preferred font requirements*/
}
.sidebarItem h3 {
    padding:8px 10px 6px 15px;
    margin-bottom:8px;
    /*be sure to set your
    preferred font requirements*/
    background:url(../images/top-side.gif) top left no-repeat;
}
```

You'll see the XHTML markup is now greatly simplified because I take advantage of my header tag as well:

```
<div class="sidebarItem"> <!--//bot-side.gif-->
    <h3>Header</h3><!--//top-side.gif-->
    Content the Template Tag outputs goes in here
</div>
```

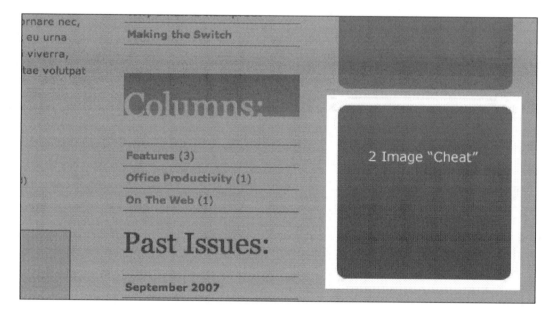

Great for block quotes! I also use this technique to handle custom block quotes that get used inside static pages and posts (a great way to spice up pages so that they look 'magazine-ish'). Again, the block quotes must be a set width, but I then only need to make sure I place in my <blockquote> and <h3> tags to have an effective style with minimal (and semantic) markup. Just replace the .sidebarItem{... from the preceding code with blockquote{... (or make a special class to assign to your <blockquote> tag).

Creative Posting

In these next few sections, we're going to focus more on ideas than specific techniques. The good news is, because you're using the Firefox browser with the Web Developer Toolbar, you'll be able to easily 'deconstruct' many of these site samples using the **CSS | View Style Information** and **CSS | View CSS** tools and think of ways to creatively use them in your own themes.

How Toons (http://www.howtoons.com/blog/) is a great kid's site that teaches them interesting things in math, art, history, and science using fun comic illustrations. The site's blog features a great use of the Comic Sans font (we discussed in Chapter 2 how it's hard to make that font *work* well; here it's perfect), and the site's author has created a very unique post template.

If you explore this site with your Web Developer Toolbar, you'll see the author creates these posts using actual image tags inside the .blogpost class. It works, and it allows the author to easily randomly assign bottom speech-bubble images with different cartoon scenes.

I'd like to point out that while the author's technique works very well, using a variation of the 'two image cheat' listed previously could achieve the same effect. This would work best if you didn't want to have randomly different post bottoms on each post. The point is, as you surf the web, you'll find there are many ways to achieve the same effect. You'll need to decide which solutions work best for you and your theme.

Breaking Boundaries

The HowToons.com site does something more than just make their posts creative; the speech-bubble bottoms of each post and the nice big background image that is positioned with `no-repeat` and `fixed` in the `bottom right`, achieve what I refer to as 'boundary breaking'.

Whether we realise it or not, we tend to create theme designs and page templates that adhere to a 'grid' of some sort. This is not a bad thing. It makes for good design, easier use of the interface, and most importantly, easier content reading.

However, I tend to find we can become 'desensitised' to many site's designs, and thus, it's interesting when a site's design displays clever ways of breaking out of the layout's grid.

Whenever I see boundary breaking done on other sites, I find it catches my eye and awakens it to really move around and take in the other details of the site's design that I might have otherwise ignored. As a result, I look for interesting ways to do this subtly within my own designs.

Within this book's case study, the OpenSource Magazine theme, I achieved this in the main and internal headers by extending it out past the `container2` div. The graphic seems to swoop back to line up with the container2 div's boundary for easy content reading, but the header extends past it, engaging the reader in a little design detail:

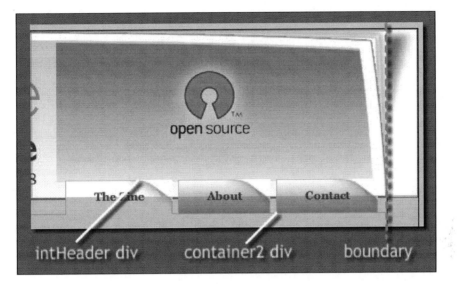

Kaushal Sheth has created a WordPress theme based on his favorite book, **The Hobbit** (`http://www.kaushalsheth.com/the-hobbit-wordpress-theme-released/`). His use of Bilbo's sword in the upper-left corner adds a nice layered dimension to the theme and interests your eye in moving around taking in all the other very nice details that Kashual took the time to put into it—the detailed paisley corners, the 'elvish' writing separating the posts, and so on.

Kaushal achieved this effect by splitting the sword and title graphic into two parts, then using an absolute positioned div to lay the handle of the sword up against the part of the image contained inside the header div.

The left side of the image is opaque, so he had to pay very special attention, making sure the absolute positioning of the div not only aligned it with the rest of the header image but also overlaid the repeating background image perfectly.

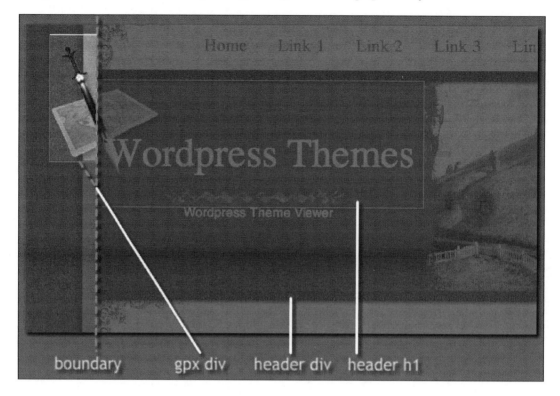

A minor drawback to the Hobbit theme is that on some browsers, while the handle of the sword is always aligned perfectly with the header h1 background image, the delicate paisley background doesn't always overlay perfectly with the site's repeating background, and as a result, you're made aware of the images edges against the background.

Rhodia Drive (http://rhodiadrive.com/) uses a similar technique to Kaushal's by using an absolute positioned div to hold a CSS background image of an orange Rhodia notebook, which breaks the boundaries on the left side. Because the site's main background uses a subtle repeat-x gradient that has been set to fixed, the image uses a **transparent PNG**. This way, as you scroll the blog up, the background of the notebook reveals the site's true background gradient.

notepad div boundary

Using transparent PNGs: The great news is IE7, and all newer browsers, natively support transparent PNGs. For the fewer out there still clinging to IE6, there's a good IE6 fix which helps that browser display transparent PNGs properly using a Microsoft filter that can be accessed via image tags and stylesheets.

The Rhodia Drive site makes use of alternate stylesheets using the `<!-- [if IE6]>` solution discussed in Chapter 4, and an IF6 transparent PNG fix, which you can find out more about at: `http://www.howtocreate.co.uk/alpha.html`.

Want to really break the boundaries? Molly E. Holzschlag has an in-depth article that goes way beyond the occasional 'overstepped line'. With pure CSS, anything is possible and it's a great thought-provoking read.

`http://www.alistapart.com/articles/outsidethegrid/`

Keep Tabs on Current Design Trends

In addition to rounded corners there are some fairly common graphic interface techniques that seem to define those trendy '2.0' sites. These include things like the following:

- **Gradients and glows**: But remember, it's all about being subtle!

- **Reflections**: Again, just be subtle!

- **Vector images and creative drop-shadows**: Give your page a feeling of space.'

- **Thin, diagonally stripped background**: Could be for just header delineation, not necessarily the whole site's background!

- **Glass or 'jelly' buttons and star-burst 'stickers'**.

- **Grunge-organic**: Emerged in its hey-day of print design in the early 90s, but it's quickly becoming the new 'shiney, clean, and bright' of Web 2.0 sites: paper-looking photos, X-File-ish folder/messy desk layouts, decaying/misprinted fonts, natural edges, and liberal (but again, subtle) doses of various spills, drips-and-drops that we usually encounter in creative life.

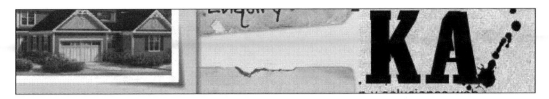

Design trends come and go; while the above are popular today, they'll become 'old hat' soon enough. Take note of bookmark leading sites and blogs of designers, web programmers, and key contributors to the web field. Visit these sites often (the good ones update their interface at least once a year; most are constantly tweaking their interface adding new things little-by-little). By keeping your finger on the 'pulse,' you'll be able to recognize new trends as they start emerging. Think about how you can creatively leverage them into your own theme designs. You'll probably find yourself inventing your own unique interface looks that other people start adopting.

Learn the ins and outs of how to use your image editing software. Right now, a large part of these design trends are graphics loaded in via CSS. To get those great trendy images into your theme, you'll need to understand CSS, and as I've already mentioned, you'll need to know how to effectively (and sometimes creatively) use the background property in your CSS rules.

PSDTuts is a *great* site for picking up a little quick 'how to' knowledge for current design techniques. The whole site is definitely worth a look through, but they have a special section for interfaces that covers how to create many design trends and visual effects using Adobe Photoshop:

`http://psdtuts.com/category/interface-tutorials/`

Stylegala and SmashingMagazine are other good sources of keeping up on web design trends. Stylegala also has a great, clear, concise CSS reference chart that I've found very useful from time to time:

`http://www.stylegala.com/features/css-reference/`

`http://smashingmagazine.com`

Graphic Text

Now here's something that's a total pain all web designers have had to deal with. As we discussed in detail in Chapter 2, there's really only three, maybe five, truly safe fonts for the web—fonts that you can be fairly sure that every PC and Mac (and maybe Linux) computer has natively installed. All other fonts tend to be off limits for web design. This is a shame, as typography is a huge element of great design. None-the-less, if you want these fonts, you have to create them as graphics and include the images into your layout.

The problem with using graphics instead of text is that it really messes with your site's semantics. Usually, it's the section headers that you want in the pretty font. However, if you use in-line image tags, your semantic markup gets thrown off and your SEO will fall because search engine bots really like to find those h1, h2, and h3 header tags to help them assess the real keywords in your page. Plus, if your style aesthetic changes, you have to not only change the theme but then update individual posts and pages with new images from within WordPress's Administration Panel.

The solution is to use text in your header tags, yet display unique fonts as images, by setting up custom classes in your stylesheet that will 'move' the text out of the way and insert your graphic font as a background image.

Again, as we mentioned in Chapter 4: search engine bots generally view your pages as though the stylesheet has been turned off, therefore the search engine bot and people using screen readers will keep flowing smoothly over pure text, while the rest of us get to see your sweet design and nice font selection. The bonus: when the site design changes, all your images are handled via the CSS sheet, so you won't have to touch individual post and static pages.

My WordPress theme makes use of Futura in the header. I'd love to use it for my section headers, the problem is, a lot of people don't have Futura on their computer. Even if my user has Futura on his machine, I think the font looks best when it's anti-aliased. While Mac users with Futura would then see it OK, PC users won't. I've created graphics of my headers using Futura, and will set up my header tags with classes to move the XHTML text out of the way and use my new background images.

> **The drawback**: Try to keep track of the bandwidth your site needs to load. The more images and the bigger they are, of course the longer it will take to load. By switching my headers from XHTML text with a small, thin repeating background, to a full non-repeating image, I went from a 1k graphic to a 10k graphic. On the whole, especially in this day and age of broadband, it's no big deal, but still something to keep in mind as you try to assess what elements of your design will use pure XHTML and CSS and what will be images.

As an example, in your CSS page, set up the following class rules:

```
.textMove{ /*this is your standard for each header*/
height: 23px;
margin-top:10px;
width: 145px;
text-indent: -2000px;/*This pushes your text back so it's invisible*/
```

```
}
.specificText{ /*specific header-text image*/
  background: url("../images/specificText.jpg") no-repeat left top;
}
```

Now, either in your theme's template pages or in posts and pages you've added via the Administration Panel, apply the appropriate classes to the text headers that you would like replaced with graphics (again, if you're in the Administration Panel, use the **Code** view).

```
<h2 class="textMove specificText">Section Header</h2>
```

Assign more than one class rule to an XHTML markup object? As you can see by our sample above, you can assign more than one class rule to a markup object. Simply separate each class rule with a *space* (not a comma), e.g., class="rule1 rule2". This comes in handy when you need to customize many elements, yet don't want to repeatedly copy similar properties across all of them (plus, you can easily change the main properties in just one spot instead of having to fix them all). In the case of graphic text headers, I like to make one rule that handles pushing the text out of the way and sets the height and margins for my header images, then, all my other class rules just handle the background image name, e.g., class="textMove graphicText". This trick *only* works with CSS *class* rules, not id rules.

Extra Credit – Use PHP to make Graphic Headers Easy

I like to simplify this process by using a simple PHP script with a local TTF font (True-Type Font) to help me quickly generate my header graphics. I can then just include them into my CSS sheet, dynamically setting up the text that the header needs to say.

This technique is very useful if your site is going to be mainly controlled by a client. As they'll probably have to let you know every time they make a new header that needs to be a graphic loaded in via CSS. You'll be able to accommodate them on-the-fly (or even better, teach them how to do it), as opposed to having them wait for you to generate the graphic with PhotoShop or Gimp, and then implement the CSS.

 Heads up: This PHP code requires the standard **ImageGD library** to be installed with your PHP configuration. This library has been on most shared/virtual hosting companies I've used, but to be safe, contact your website host administrator to ensure the ImageGD library is installed.

You can place this script's file anywhere you'd like. I usually place it in my theme's image directory — imgtxt.php — as I will be referencing it as an image.

```
<?PHP
/*Basic JPG creator by Tessa Blakeley Silver
Free to use and change. No warranty.
Author assumes no liability, use at own risk.*/
header("Content-type: image/jpeg");

$xspan = $_REQUEST['xspan'];//if you want to adjust the width
$wrd = $_REQUEST['wrd'];//what the text is
if (!$xspan){//set a default width
    $xspan = 145;
}
$height = 20;//set a default height
$image = imagecreate($xspan, $height);
//Set your background color.
//set to what ever rgb color you want
if(!$bckCol){
    $bckCol = imagecolorallocate($image, 255, 255, 255);
}
//make text color, again set to what ever rgb color you want
if (!$txtCol){
    $txtCol = imagecolorallocate($image, 20, 50, 150);
```

```
}
//fill background
imagefilledrectangle($image, 0, 0, $xspan, $height, $bckCol);

//set the font size on the 2nd parameter in
//set the server path (not the url path!) to the font location at the
7th parameter in:
imagettftext($image, 15, 0, 0, 16, $txtCol, "home/user/sitename/fonts/
PLANE____.TTF", "$wrd");//add text

imagejpeg($image,'',80);//the last number sets the jpg compression

//free up the memory allocated for the image.
imagedestroy($image);

?>
```

This script only works with **True-Type fonts**. Upload the True-Type font and directory location you referenced in the script to the matching location on the server. Also, my script is very basic, no drop-shadows or reflections. It only creates a JPG with a solid background color, True-Type font, font-size, and solid font color. If you're comfortable with PHP, you can Google/search the web for PHP image scripts that allow you to do more with your text-image, that is, add gradient backgrounds or generate transparent PNGs, or overlay other images on top of or behind your text.

From here on out, you'll only need to reference this PHP script in your CSS, passing your text to it via a query string instead of the images you were generating:

```
.specificText {
    background: url("../images/imgtxt.php?xspan=300&wrd=
            This Is My New Text") no-repeat left top;
}
```

The xspan variable is optional; if you don't include it, the default in the script is set to 145 pixels wide. If your custom text will be longer than 145 pixels, you can set it to the pixel width you desire. (In the previous example, I have it set to 300. Be sure your width doesn't conflict with your div widths!)

The wrd variable is where you'll set your custom text. (Be aware that some characters may not come over as the string will be url encoded.)

Each time you have a new graphic to generate, you can do it entirely via the theme's stylesheet. The following is a screenshot from my professional site, which uses the PHP script in the previous example to generate header fonts.

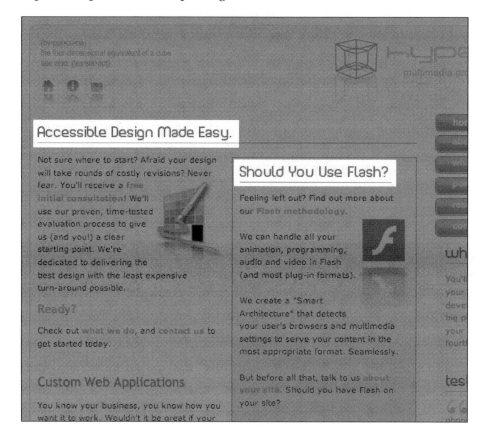

Good Design isn't Always Visual – Looking at SEO

At this point you've gone through the trouble to create a semantic, user-friendly, and accessible XHTML theme, and one of the benefits of that structure is that it helps with SEO (Search Engine Optimization, if you haven't guessed by now). You might as well go all out and take time to set up a few more optimizations.

Search Engine Friendly URLs

WordPress URLs by default are dynamic. That means they are a query string of the `index.php` page, e.g, `http://mysite.com/?p=123`.

In the past, dynamic URLs had been known to break search engine bots who either didn't know what to do when they hit a question mark or ampersand and/or started indexing entire sites as 'duplicate content', because everything looked like it was coming from the same page (usually the `index.php` page).

Generally, this is *no longer the case*, at least not with the 'big boy' search engines like Google, but you never know who is searching for you using what service.

Also, by changing the dynamic string URL to a more SEF (Search Engine Friendly) URL, it's a little harder for people to directly manipulate your URLs because they can't clearly see what variable they're changing once it's in a search engine friendly URL.

WordPress has this SEF URL feature built-in, but *only* if you're running PHP on Apache.

Go to **Adiministration | Settings | Permalinks (Administration | Options | Permalinks** in version **2.3.x)** and simply switch the **Default** selection to either **Day and Name** based, **Numeric**, or **Custom**.

I like to select **Custom** and tell my structure to be /%category%/%postname%/. That way, my URLs will reflect the category they are posted to and then the permalink title which is your post's title with (-) dashes put in for spaces. If your blog is going to be more date-based, then one of the presets might be a better option for you.

Customize Permalink Structure

By default WordPress uses web URLs which have question marks and lots of numbers in them, ho‍ URL structure for your permalinks and archives. This can improve the aesthetics, usability, and fo‍ available, and here are some examples to get you started.

Common settings

⊙ **Default**	http://wpdev25.eternalurbanyouth.com/?p=123	
⊙ **Day and name**	http://wpdev25.eternalurbanyouth.com/2008/04/02/sample-post/	
⊙ **Month and name**	http://wpdev25.eternalurbanyouth.com/2008/04/sample-post/	
⊙ **Numeric**	http://wpdev25.eternalurbanyouth.com/archives/123	
⊙ **Custom Structure**	/%year%/%monthnum%/%category%/%postname%/	

Optional

If you like, you may enter custom structures for your category and tag URLs here. For example, us‍ category links like http://example.org/topics/uncategorized/. If you leave these blank th‍

Category base	/columns

Search engine bots will 'think' the forward slashes are directories and not freak out about question marks and ampersands, or assume that everything on your site is really the same page.

Forget the Search Engine Friendly! What about People-Friendly URLs?
WordPress is great at people-friendly URLs. Comprehensive URLs are one of the great things about WordPress **2**, and a feature that places it above other comparable CMS and blog tools currently out there (even if you select 'SEF' URLs, it can still be a long URL of odd numbers and incomprehensible variable names separated by slashes).

Sometimes, you're in a situation where you just can't copy and paste your link over! It's great to have lunch with your friend and be able to *verbally* give her the URL to your latest web-rant and know that she'll easily remember: `http://myurl.com/rants/newrant`. Also, clearly named URLs greatly boost your "link trust" (that's what I call it anyway). If the relevant link you've emailed people or posted in your blog, or as a comment on someone elses blog doesn't appear to clearly have any indication of what you promised is in it, people are much less likely to click on it (do you like clicking on long strings of odd numbers and cryptic variable names?). And, while the impact of key words in URLs seems to be waning, there are SEO experts who still swear that your URLs should contain the top key words in your document. If you haven't done so already, be sure to take advantage of this feature in WordPress.

Keywords and Descriptions

Most people just 'hard code' some general keyword and description metatags into their theme's template files that best describe the overall gist of their WordPress site. However, if you want to aid in your content being indexed by search engines a little better and/or you use your WordPress site to cover a wide range of diverse information which an overall gist of keywords and a description just won't cover, you'll want to make metatags in your template files a bit more dynamic. There are several ways in which you can add keyword and description metatags for individual posts and pages to your WordPress theme. You can use the available template tags within your theme's `index.php` or `header.php` pages to add content to your metatags, or you can install third-party plug-ins which will expand your administration page options and give you a little more control than what is produced by your post's content.

DYI Metatags

For most people, myself included, this method works well. In my `index.php` and `header.php` template files, I set up my metatags for keywords and descriptions. I then take advantage of the `single_cat_title()`, `single_post_title()`, and `the_exerpt()` template tags.

In my keywords metatag, I include the `single_cat_title()` and then the `single_post_title()` tags like as follows:

```
<meta name="keywords" content="<?echo single_cat_title('');?>, <?echo
single_post_title('');?>" />
```

The previous modification will give my page the following runtime output:

```
<meta name="keywords" content="Office Productivity, Fun with OO2" />
```

This, if you keep keywords in mind while writing your titles and assigning them to categories, will be fairly comprehensive.

Setting up the description tag takes just a bit more, as `the_exerpt()` tag only works within The Loop. So you just need to make sure you set up a little 'mini loop' for it to run in, like so:

```
<meta name="description" content="
<? if(is_category() || is_archive()) {
    echo the_excerpt();
  } else {
    echo 'This is my default description to use if a post or page
doesn't have an excerpt';
  } ?>
" />
```

The previous code will produce a description that looks like the following:

```
<meta name="description" content="This is the optional excerpt for
this article, Fun with OO2. I use the Optional Excerpt field to aid in
my description metatags." />
```

Metatag Plug-ins

If you're a serious blogger and really need more robust options for your metatags, you might want to try one of the following two WordPress plug-ins:

- **All in One SEO Pack** by uberdose 2.0 (`http://wp.uberdose.com/2007/03/24/all-in-one-seo-pack/`). This plug-in utilizes the `the_exerpt()` tag as we just did, but also allows you to set your own specific keywords and several other great options for handling robust metatag information for each post.

- **Ultimate Tag Warrior 3** by neato.co.nz (`http://www.neato.co.nz/ultimate-tag-warrior/`). This plug-in doesn't do so well with the metatag description, but for the really 'hard core' out there who want to ensure their keyword usage is maximized, this seems to be the plug-in of choice. It includes a Yahoo! keyword suggestor, which informs you what words Yahoo! has deemed important in your post.

Summary

We've reviewed the main tips you should have picked up from the previous chapters, and covered some key tips for easily implementing today's coolest CSS tricks into your theme, as well as a few final SEO tips that you'll probably run into once you really start putting content into your site, or turn the site over to the content editors. I hope you've enjoyed this book and found it useful in aiding your WordPress theme creations.

Index

Packt Open Source Project Royalties

When we sell a book written on an Open Source project, we pay a royalty directly to that project. Therefore by purchasing WordPress Theme Design, Packt will have given some of the money received to the WordPress project.

In the long term, we see ourselves and you — customers and readers of our books — as part of the Open Source ecosystem, providing sustainable revenue for the projects we publish on. Our aim at Packt is to establish publishing royalties as an essential part of the service and support a business model that sustains Open Source.

If you're working with an Open Source project that you would like us to publish on, and subsequently pay royalties to, please get in touch with us.

Writing for Packt

We welcome all inquiries from people who are interested in authoring. Book proposals should be sent to authors@packtpub.com. If your book idea is still at an early stage and you would like to discuss it first before writing a formal book proposal, contact us; one of our commissioning editors will get in touch with you.

We're not just looking for published authors; if you have strong technical skills but no writing experience, our experienced editors can help you develop a writing career, or simply get some additional reward for your expertise.

About Packt Publishing

Packt, pronounced 'packed', published its first book "Mastering phpMyAdmin for Effective MySQL Management" in April 2004 and subsequently continued to specialize in publishing highly focused books on specific technologies and solutions.

Our books and publications share the experiences of your fellow IT professionals in adapting and customizing today's systems, applications, and frameworks. Our solution-based books give you the knowledge and power to customize the software and technologies you're using to get the job done. Packt books are more specific and less general than the IT books you have seen in the past. Our unique business model allows us to bring you more focused information, giving you more of what you need to know, and less of what you don't.

Packt is a modern, yet unique publishing company, which focuses on producing quality, cutting-edge books for communities of developers, administrators, and newbies alike. For more information, please visit our website: www.PacktPub.com.

WordPress Complete

ISBN: 978-1-904811-89-3   Paperback: 272 pages

A comprehensive, step-by-step guide on how to set up, customize, and market your blog using WordPress

1. Clear practical coverage of all aspects of WordPress

2. Concise, clear, and easy to follow, rich with examples

3. In-depth coverage of installation, themes, syndication, and podcasting

Joomla! Template Design

ISBN: 978-1-847191-44-1   Paperback: 250 pages

A complete guide for web designers to all aspects of designing unique website templates for the free Joomla! 1.0.8 PHP Content Management System

1. Create Joomla! Templates for your sites

2. Debug, validate, and package your templates

3. Tips for tweaking existing templates

Please check **www.PacktPub.com** for information on our titles

DATE

2941263

Made in the USA